Life Skills Instruction for All Students With Special Needs
A Practical Guide for Integrating Real-Life Content Into the Curriculum

Life Skills Instruction for All Students With Special Needs

A Practical Guide for Integrating Real-Life Content Into the Curriculum

Mary E. Cronin

James R. Patton

pro·ed

8700 Shoal Creek Boulevard
Austin, Texas 78757

pro·ed

© 1993 by PRO-ED, Inc.
8700 Shoal Creek Boulevard
Austin, Texas 78757-6897

Library of Congress Cataloging-in-Publication Data

Cronin, Mary E.
    Life skills instruction for all students with special needs : a
practical guide for integrating real-life content into the
curriculum / Mary E. Cronin, James R. Patton.
        p.   cm.
    Includes bibliographical references and index.
    ISBN 0-89079-586-X
    1. Handicapped children—United States—life skills guides.
2. Life skills—Study and teaching—United States. I. Patton,
James R.   II. Title.
HV888.5.C76   1993
371.9—dc20   92-40196
                                                CIP

This book is designed in Cheltenham Book, with Futura.

Production Manager: Alan Grimes
Production Coordinator: Adrienne Booth
Art Director: Lori Kopp
Reprints Buyer: Alicia Woods
Editor: Amy Root
Editorial Assistant: Claudette Landry

Printed in the United States of America

1 2 3 4 5 6 7 8 9 10   97 96 95 94 93

Contents

Tables and Figures by Chapters

Preface

As we have experienced adulthood, we have come to recognize the complexities of dealing successfully with the demanding responsibilities that befall us. Much of the time, we have dealt with these demands in appropriate ways; sometimes, we have failed miserably. However, we continue to learn all of the time!

The importance of being prepared for various adult challenges was made clear to us when the first child of one of the authors was born. Such an event presents many opportunities to demonstrate competence in a range of areas. For example, within four days of the child's birth, it was necessary to administer a suppository to her. It's difficult to imagine that one would have to do this at all—much less to such a small creature. It became apparent that this skill as well as a whole set of other specific life skills for dealing with a newborn infant were never taught formally and unfortunately were never learned incidentally either. Suffice it to say that the cognitive study of life skills does not necessarily prepare one for performing any of them successfully.

We consider ourselves educated folks and know, for the most part, how to exercise good common sense. We often wonder how others, many of whom do not have the resources that we have, cope with the demands of daily living. Having been special-education teachers, we especially wonder how students who have limited support systems and an array of special needs, and who have not shown great skills in picking things up incidentally from their environments, deal with the stresses as well as the pleasures of life.

This guide was inspired by many different motivations. Our combined teaching experiences and reflections on the frustrations we felt in preparing students for what happened to them upon exiting school were significant factors. First-hand experience in developing and implementing a life skills curriculum in pilot classrooms in Louisiana's Jefferson and St. Bernard Parishes, along with discussions with many classroom teachers, convinced both authors that teachers needed a practical guide to help them cover life skills topics.

We feel strongly that all students—whether they have special needs or not—need to be presented opportunities to acquire requisite life skills. Because we have seen many students prosper from being taught these skills, we decided to develop a guide that would provide anyone interested in teaching life skills with (1) a procedure for doing so; (2) suggestions for making the task more successful; and (3) lists of resources for making the endeavor less time-intensive.

We hope you will find this material user-friendly. We have tried to organize it in such a manner that users can find information and topics easily. We like to think that this book is worth adding to one's professional library under the "practical resource" category.

We do not claim that this is the definitive work on life skills—it is only a guide to developing locally referenced and culturally responsive programs. In our opinion, quality life skills programs are not found in books like this; they are developed at the local level by professionals who are keenly aware of their students' needs. We hope that we can be of some assistance to those who feel as strongly as we do that students need to be prepared for the real world.

Over the years we have been fortunate to get to know professionals such as Gary Clark, Don Brolin, Gene Edgar, and their colleagues who have had a major impact on our thinking and motivated us to continue the struggle. For years, these folks have been championing the need to teach functional skills and offer innovative curricular options. Their professional contributions (writings and curricular materials) as well as the work of others to whom we apologize for failing to mention by name, have directly or indirectly benefited many students with special needs. We only hope that we can do the same.

Personnel of schools systems in Louisiana, Texas, and Iowa need to be recognized for their willingness to try something innovative and for their ongoing support of our efforts. In the early years, Barbara Turner, Mary Carlton, Barbara Speigal, Dan Webre, and Marla Seelig of Jefferson Parish, and Janice Campagna, Michelle Crosby, Ronnie Palmisano, Deborah Lord, Kathy Wendling, Michele Burmaster, and Lena Blaise of St. Bernard Parish, and Nancy Hicks of the Special Education Department of the State of Louisiana were all significant players in addressing the life skills needs of many students. In recent times, Donald Moeker and Nola Hamlin of Temple Texas Independent School District and Lynn Helmke of Dubuque Community School District (Iowa) have implemented draft forms of our life skills model in various ways.

We would be negligent if we did not recognize the Adult Performance Level (APL) Project of The University of Texas at Austin for the initial work in the 1970s that led to an adaptation of the model for students with mild disabilities. The adaptation and modification project was spearheaded by Ann LaQuey, who is now with the Region XIII Service Center in Austin and greatly influenced many of our early conceptualizations of life skills.

We want to acknowledge some other people to whom we owe a great deal of thanks. We want to thank Cindy Bechtel for her many hours of assistance making this guide a reality. Without her, it would still be only a dream. We also want to thank Joan Clum, Sonya Yates, Cindy Andress, Rebecca Fletcher, and Gwenn Long for their involvement in various aspects of this project. We would also like to acknowledge Patricia Sitlington, Linda Brown, and the Zimmermans—Janet, Sey, Patrick, Thomas, and Frank—for their encouragement and constant interest. We also want to give special thanks to the production folks at PRO-ED—Alan Grimes, Lori Kopp, and Adrienne Booth—for their expertise in guiding this work through the hoops and for making the final product look so good. We want to thank Amy Root, who diligently copyedited the manuscript.

We also want to express our gratitude to our spouses, Stuart Dixon and Joy Kataoka, for putting up with all of the meetings needed to pull this off. Our work on this project necessitated much travel and time away from family; we are acutely aware of how invaluable support systems are. Lastly, we want to let Kimi know that she provided many pleasurable moments and reality checks for us during this endeavor.

To Stuart, Joy, and Kimi

The Importance of Life Skills Instruction for All Students With Special Needs

The schooling experience is designed to prepare individuals for adulthood, essentially to create a competent citizenry. In the early school years, students are taught basic skills that they will use in applied ways in subsequent school endeavors and ultimately in life. The mastery of the scholastic skills of reading, writing, and performing mathematical tasks are the *sine qua non* for a literate society. Their relevance in terms of career and personal independence is extremely important, resulting in these skills being the foundation upon which our schooling experience is based.

Many other skills and areas of knowledge are extremely valuable but are not fundamental academic skills or the type of content knowledge covered in the traditional curriculum. Many skills needed to get by in today's world do not involve knowledge of the periodic table or the use of various trigonometric functions; instead, they involve the ability to handle the events that we all encounter on a day-to-day basis. (Chapter 2 identifies 146 major demands of adulthood.) For the most part, current school programs do not prepare students for the array of day-to-day challenges that most of us face as adults.

This guide provides procedures and suggestions for covering life skills topics in which students with special needs must display competence to successfully deal with adulthood. The conceptual framework of the guide derives from a realistic appraisal of likely subsequent environments for students and applying a top-down process to curriculum development. In other words, the scope and sequence of what should be taught to students with special needs must be predicated on a thorough examination of the demands of adulthood that these students are likely to face. In the oppositional bottom-up approach, curricular content is arbitrarily selected with the expectation that it will benefit students in their future living and work environments.

While we believe that this guide is appropriate for all students, regardless of any identifiable specific need, we use the term "students with special needs" throughout the guide. We are referring to individuals who are at risk either for not doing well in school-related tasks or for having difficulty dealing with the demands of daily living. This might include individuals who have disabilities, are low-achieving, require alternative learning conditions, or come from environments that limit their opportunities for success.

BACKGROUND

Recent concern for what happens to students when formal schooling ends has focused on two principal areas: the adult outcome data of students who were formerly in special education and the dropout data on students with special needs. This section will briefly review the findings and implications related to these two areas.

Adult Outcome Data

During the 1980s some key follow-up studies (Affleck, Edgar, Levine, & Kortering, 1990; Blackorby, Edgar, & Kortering, 1991; Edgar, 1987; Hasazi, Gordon, & Roe, 1985; Mithaug, Horiuchi, & Fanning, 1985; White, Alley, Deshler, Schumaker, Warner, & Clark, 1982) were conducted. Although the data from these studies were collected in different parts of the country, sometimes focused on different groups of students with special needs, and showed some intersite variations, the general findings suggested a less-than-favorable scenario for these young adults. Many of these young adults' lives were often associated with unemployment and/or underemployment, low pay, part-time work, frequent job changes, nonengagement with the community, limited independent functioning, and restricted social lives.

These studies, as well as others conducted locally by school districts throughout the country, have had a significant impact on current thinking and professional discussion. However, for a number of reasons they provide only a partial picture of the lives and resultant problems facing many adults. First, most of the research provides a "snapshot" (i.e., at one point in time) of the lives (i.e., outcomes) of young adults. As a result, little information exists on the impact that their special needs have on the quality of their lives. This is due to the simple fact that this type of research can be methodologically problematic, expensive, and effort-intensive. Yet, the need to obtain a longitudinal sense of how these adults cope with the demands of adulthood remains an important and relatively untapped area for research activity (Gajar, 1992).

Second, most studies conducted to date examine a restricted range of outcome measures, usually focusing on employment and other general demographic dimensions (e.g., marital status). Omitted are measures of performance on day-to-day facets of adulthood such as managing money, getting along with one's spouse, or utilizing community services. Perhaps even more important, little information has been collected on various qualitative

aspects of adulthood such as one's values, happiness, well-being, and goals. These omissions—similar to those made for the lack of longitudinal studies—result from the fact that gathering this type of information is difficult, expensive, and time-consuming.

Exit Data

The second major source of concern for professionals centers on the various ways students in special education "exit" from the school system. National data for the 1989–90 school year on the exit status of former students identified as mentally retarded, learning disabled, or emotionally disturbed are reported in the *Fourteenth Annual Report to Congress on the Implementation of Individuals with Disabilities Education Act* (U.S. Department of Education, 1992) are presented in Table 1.1.

It is important to note that the "real dropout" data category is not an official category in the Office of Special Education Programs (OSEP) report, as it is a derived figure comprising the "actual dropout" counts and the "unknown exit" data. It is a valuable numeric because it provides a more realistic indication of the problem associated with students (i.e., in this case, students with these types of disabilities) leaving school prior to finishing their programs. Although it is possible that students who are in this "unknown exit" category may re-enroll at a later time to further their education and may ultimately finish school, it is more likely that they will simply drop out and never receive any additional education.

As can be seen in Table 1.1, there are obvious differences across the three groups. It is significant that the potential dropout rates are substantial for these particular groups: mental retardation = 31%; learning disability = 38%; emotional disturbance = 60%. These figures only illustrate the problem, as these groups represent some of the students considered as having special needs.

Implications

Based on the research on adult outcomes and exit status of students, Cronin, Patton, and Polloway (1991) conclude that

TABLE 1.1. Exit Data on Select Students With Special Needs (For 1989–90 Year)

Exit Basis	Mental Retardation	Learning Disabilities	Emotional Disturbance
Diploma	37.5%	51.9%	30.7%
Certificate	24.4	10.0	6.1
Age-Out	6.7	.5	2.2
Dropout	23.6	26.8	43.2
Unknown Exit	7.8	10.9	17.8
Real Dropout	31.4	37.7	60.0

Source: U.S. Department of Education. (1992). *Fourteenth annual report to Congress on the implementation of the Individuals with Disabilities Education Act.* Washington, DC: Office of Special Education Programs, Office of Special Education and Rehabilitative Services.

- Many individuals with special needs are not being prepared for the multidimensional demands of adulthood;

- A large percentage of students who have special needs are not finding the school experience to be valuable and are dropping out;

- The educational programs of many students are not meeting their current and future needs;

- The provision of continuing-education options (i.e., recruitment, ongoing support, specialized training, and follow-up services) for adults with special needs is warranted;

- There is a pressing need, therefore, to re-examine school curriculum at both secondary and elementary levels, possibly leading to innovative ways to address the functional needs of students in addition to the traditional academic needs.

All students need to acquire those life skills necessary for successfully dealing with everyday living (i.e., productive adulthood). Unfortunately, a very small number of functional life skills are actually addressed in the traditional curricula found in most schools, and, if covered at all, are taught in classrooms rather than in applied community settings (Halpern, Benz, & Lindstrom, 1992). Many individuals do learn specific life skills on their own along the way in nonformal ways or from family and friends; many others do not. The stakes are too high to leave this area of learning to chance.

In light of the realities highlighted above, efforts are warranted to find ways to teach important life skills to students at risk for failing or dropping out of school as well as to students who will stay in school but need the competencies to deal with their future worlds. The next section discusses the nature of existing curricular offerings found in schools today.

EXISTING CURRICULAR OFFERINGS

Upon inspection of school curricula, it is possible to draw some conclusions that tend to represent the nature of the content that is being taught in schools today. This section will highlight the curricular features of elementary and secondary curriculum and offer some salient arguments for curricular innovation.

Grade-Level Distinctions

Elementary level. In general, the focus of the curriculum for all students at the elementary level is the development and mastery of basic skills. As students progress through the upper elementary grades, emphasis is put on using these skills in more applied ways. In essence, these skills are being refined so that students can handle the growing amount of content knowledge being introduced and deal effectively with increasingly more complex demands associated with secondary-level coursework. For some students who are in special education, more time is likely to be devoted to remediation of the basic skills that have not been acquired.

Although providing career education at this level is warranted and advocated strongly (Clark, Carlson, Fisher, Cook, & D'Alonzo, 1991), in reality, little instruction occurs (Moore, Agran, & McSweyn,

1990). Covering career education with elementary-aged students provides a valuable linkage with transitional activities that must occur at the secondary levels. Such instruction can cover topics that are precursors to life skills that can be taught at a later time. Clark and colleagues offer the following principles:

- Education for career development and transition is for individuals with disabilities at all ages.

- Career development is a process begun at birth and continues throughout life.

- Early career development is essential for making satisfactory choices later.

- Significant gaps or periods of neglect in any area of basic human development affects career development and the transition from one stage of life to another.

- Career development is responsive to intervention and programming, when the programming involves direct instruction for individual needs.

Teaching career education obviously has direct relevance to the development of life skills. As chapter 3 will discuss, a comprehensive conceptualization of life skills instruction extends the preparation for adulthood down to the elementary level.

Secondary level. Curricular orientation at the secondary level, particularly for students with special needs, can be more clearly specified. A number of professionals (Polloway, Patton, Epstein, & Smith, 1989; Zigmond & Sansone, 1986) have offered different categorical arrangements for secondary curricular orientation. Much of the literature suggests three general orientations, each of which contains more specific curricular models: remedial, maintenance, and functional. Due to confusion associated with these terms and in consort with what is occuring in schools, Polloway and Patton (1993) present a modified model of curricular options. Table 1.2 provides an overview of these options, listing the major features of each specific curricular model and highlighting the functionality of each.

Need for Curricular Innovation

The appropriateness of the various curricular options described in Table 1.2 depends on a number of variables that must be considered (see Polloway et al., 1989). Nevertheless, most students with special needs will require elements from more than one of the options. We propose that all students, whether they have been identified as having special needs or not, should be provided instruction on dealing with the day-to-day demands of adulthood (i.e., life skills). For students with special needs, it is imperative that their current and future needs be considered in designing programs.

With the movement to provide the educational programs of as many students with special needs as possible in regular education settings, creative ways to deliver life skills instruction are needed. Interestingly, having this type of instruction within the regular education setting offers great benefits to all students, as there are many students in these settings who are at risk for unsuccessfully dealing with adulthood.

THE NATURE OF LIFE SKILLS INSTRUCTION

Although it is easy to make a case for teaching life skills, we note that they are not taught often enough. This guide helps professionals address that very concern. This section presents a brief look at previous initiatives supporting the development of programs that prepare students for adulthood. The section closes with a list of principles to guide those of us who are truly concerned about the best interests of students with special needs.

Historical Perspective on Teaching Functional Skills

Interest in teaching functional skills is not a new phenomenon, as many dedicated people have argued for such instruction for a long time. As Kolstoe (1976) pointed out, the goals of the National Education Association as specified in a 1938 document suggest a strong interest in functional outcomes. The goals focus on economic efficiency,

TABLE 1.2. Overview of Curricular Options

Curricular Theme	Specific Curricular Orientation	Major Features	Functional Relevance
Academic Content Coverage		• general education content taught in special settings • materials can be those used in general education or alternative ones • concern about special teacher's background to teach some content areas	• need for similar content acquisition as nondisabled peers • precursor to integration into general education classes
Remedial	*Basic Skills*	• goal is to increase academic performance to desired levels • intensive programming in reading, math, language arts • generalization of skills needs to be programmed • some programs that focus too much on this orientation may neglect other areas	• increase literacy levels • can address deficit areas so that students can be integrated into general education classes
	Social Skills	• relates to social skill development, affective needs, and behavior change needs • generalization of acquired behaviors can be a concern	• increase one's social competence • potential benefits for inclusive settings • importance of developing one's self-concept
Regular Class Support	*Tutorial Assistance*	• teacher works with student on instructional topics that have immediate relevance in the general classroom • provides a short-term emphasis on needs but may not have long-term value	• addresses immediate needs (e.g., test) for the student • serves a diplomatic function—it helps the general education teacher with students who need ongoing assistance
	Compensatory Tactics	• idea is to circumvent areas of difficulty (e.g., using a calculator when significant problems arise in this area) • techniques may not be available for all situations • typically used in conjunction with other orientations	• provides an alternate way to achieve desired goals in spite of problems
	Learning Strategies	• cognitive-based techniques that teach students how to use their abilities and knowledge to solve problems, acquire information, deal with given situations • may not be useful with all students • must be used in conjunction with other orientations if students are not in general education • important to program for transfer of skills from the training setting to others	• provides long-term tactics for dealing with similar situations • allows students to compete with peers who do not have disabilities
	Cooperative Teaching	• team approach to addressing the needs of students • special education teacher works in the general education classroom	• provides content learning and inclusion

(Table continues)

TABLE 1.2. *Continued*

Curricular Theme	Specific Curricular Orientation	Major Features	Functional Relevance
Adult Outcomes	*Vocational Training*	• focus in on the acquisition of requisite skills in a specific vocational area • variety of vocational training options are available • addresses a major component transition service requirement of Individuals with Disabilities Education Act (IDEA)	• students acquire a specific vocation skill or skills before leaving school • motivates students by providing relevance to the curriculum • shifts focus away from past failure in academic domains
	Life Skill Preparation	• acquisition of specific life skills to deal with the typical challenges of everyday life • content emphasis should be based on a realistic appraisal of what students will face when school is over • life skills can be taught in educational placement	• competency in dealing with major life demands is required of all individuals • motivates students and shifts focus away from previous failure experiences

worthy home membership, worthy citizenship, and self-realization.

Many programs of the 1950s and 1960s for students with mental retardation were designed with adult outcomes in mind. Programs heavily emphasized functional skills, particularly related to vocational training and employment. Typically, school districts developed curriculum guides with functional themes that were used extensively with students in special education.

During the 1980s, the dramatic realization that disappointing adult outcomes existed for many former students gave rise to more formal study of the youth transition from school to adult life. This realization was particularly painful, considering that many of these former students had received extensive special education services during their school careers. Even though the transition movement has focused more on linking students to adult services and enhancing the mechanisms that facilitate these linkages, some attention has been given to the curricular implications of this process (Patton, 1986).

In a more contemporary context, some confusion exists today concerning how to address the need for life skills preparation in light of the inclusive education movement whereby many students are receiving academically oriented educational programs within regular education classes. This is not a problem, but tactics for covering life skills in such settings are not obvious. Chapter 3 attempts

to show some examples of how life skill instruction can be provided to students who are in inclusive settings.

Given the realities of current restructuring in special education, certain special education professionals (Brolin, 1978; Clark, 1980; Edgar, 1987, 1988; Kortering & Elrod, 1991; Patton, Cronin, Polloway, Hutchinson, & Robinson, 1989) have argued that curricular options emphasizing the skills needed to be successful adults should be available to students. The future challenge is to balance the need for students to be in integrated, academically oriented settings with the need to provide instruction on life skills topics that they will most certainly need in their foreseeable futures.

Guiding Principles for This Book

In light of the preceding discussion on the challenges facing us, professionals concerned about the adult outcomes of youth in today's schools must identify a philosophy that guides policy, decisions, and actions. We want to share these principles that guide how we conceptualize service delivery.

- *Utilize the notion of "subsequent environment as attitude."* The concept described by Polloway, Patton, Smith, and Roderique (1991) implies that everything we do with students should be considered in the context of where they will likely be in the near future.

- *Treat each instructional day as if it were the last day in a student's scholastic life.* This idea stresses the importance of making every moment count. As many teachers know, there are students who may at any time drop out of school and will never return.

- *Re-evaluate what we are doing with students on a regular basis.* It is extremely important that we continually strive to be innovative in terms of curricular design and instructional methodology.

These three principles should apply to all educational decisions related to youth at risk. These principles certainly apply to the themes discussed in the remainder of this book.

Identification of Major Life Demands and Specific Life Skills

Given the importance of teaching life skills to students, we are faced with the challenge of identifying these skills. The purpose of this chapter is threefold: (1) to provide a framework by which to conceptualize the challenges of adulthood; (2) to identify the major demands that most students will encounter in their adult lives; and (3) to show how specific life skills that are locally referenced can be generated from an analysis of the listed major life demands.

The model used in this guide for identifying specific life skills relies on a top-down approach to content or curriculum development. This model, depicted in Figure 2.1, emphasizes the need to consider likely subsequent environments of students and basing curriculum development on working "down" from consideration of anticipated outcomes. The various major life demands required for success in different postschool environments can be organized into general domains. Ultimately, this process leads to the identification of specific life skills that can be taught to students. The remainder of this chapter describes the various components of this model in more detail.

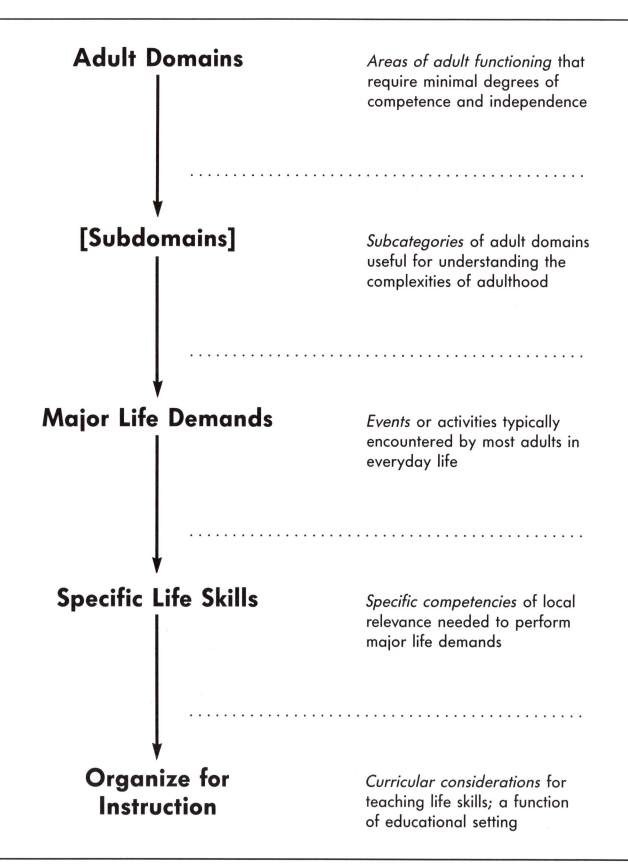

Adult Domains

Areas of adult functioning that require minimal degrees of competence and independence

[Subdomains]

Subcategories of adult domains useful for understanding the complexities of adulthood

Major Life Demands

Events or activities typically encountered by most adults in everyday life

Specific Life Skills

Specific competencies of local relevance needed to perform major life demands

Organize for Instruction

Curricular considerations for teaching life skills; a function of educational setting

Figure 2.1. Top-Down Approach to Curriculum Development.

DOMAINS OF ADULT LIFE

This section attempts to organize the various day-to-day demands of living into a useful format. Unfortunately, these demands are categorized somewhat arbitrarily. The most important criterion is that the selected domains capture the vast complexities of adulthood as best as possible.

Adult domains, as defined in Figure 2.1, are those areas of adult functioning that require minimal degrees of competence and independence. A number of sources exist where one can find formats for organizing skills deemed necessary for adult living. Table 2.1 summarizes a select list of sources for finding this information. Although all use different descriptors to refer to functional areas, they share common themes. All of these models have merit and are worth further examination.

The conceptualization of adult domains used in this guide developed out of the Hawaii Transition Project (1987). One of the early efforts of the project focused on the development of a frame of reference for looking at the transitional needs of students. Initially, nine areas of transition were identified; however, over time these nine areas were reduced to six, as indicated in Table 2.1. These six domains fell under one of two overriding areas: life domains and support domains. Patton and Browder (1988) explain the distinction between the two areas:

> The designation of life domains is simple—the domains represent how most individuals explicitly or implicitly organize their lives. The selection of support domains is likewise simple—the need to provide financially for one's food, shelter, clothing, and physical and emotional health must be met before individuals can take on adult responsibilities and activities beyond themselves. (p. 296)

TABLE 2.1. Select Conceptualizations of Adulthood Dimensions

Source	Major Functional Areas
Life Centered Career Education (LCCE) (Brolin, 1991)	22 competencies divided across three domains: • Daily Living • Personal-Social • Occupational Guidance and Preparation
Community-Referenced Curriculum (Smith & Schloss, 1988)	Major areas: • Work • Leisure and Play • Consumer • Education and Rehabilitation • Transportation
Community Living Skills Taxonomy (Dever, 1988)	Major areas: • Personal Maintenance and Development • Homemaking and Community Life • Vocational • Leisure • Travel
Life Problems of U.S. Adults (Knowles, 1990)	Major Areas: • Vocation and Career • Home and Family Living • Enjoyment of Leisure • Community Living • Health • Personal Development
Hawaii Transition Project (1987)	Four Life Domains: • Vocation/Education • Home and Family • Recreation/Leisure • Community/Citizenship (Guardianship/Advocacy) Two Support Domains: • Financial Support • Emotional/Physical Health

The life and support domains used in the Hawaii Transition Project were modified over time into a new set of general adult domains. One source that contributed to this modification was Knowles' (1990) categorization of the adult problems of young adults. The domains used in this guide are highlighted in Figure 2.2. We feel that all of the activities that we do as adults can fall into one of the six domains; the domains are closely related to the way we organize our lives.

DOMAINS OF ADULTHOOD

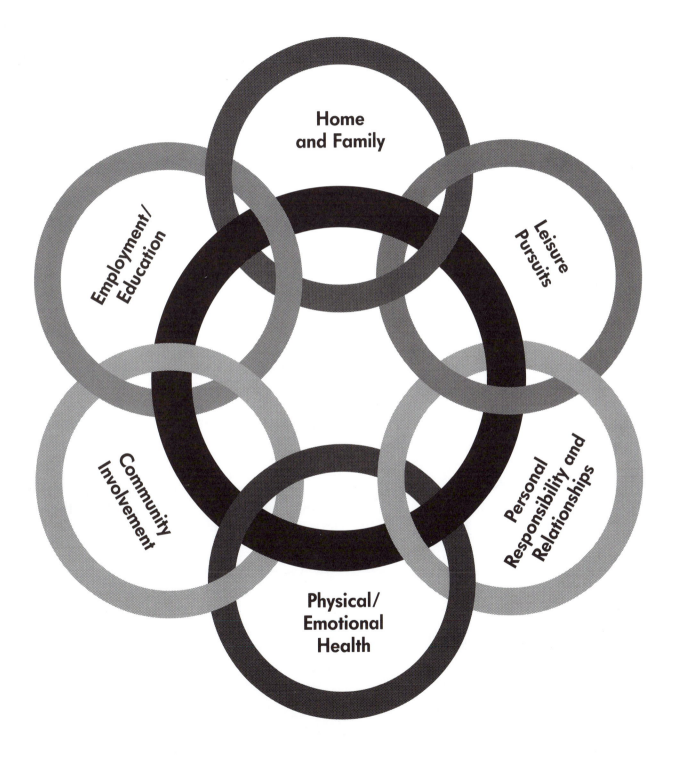

Figure 2.2. Domains of Adulthood.

To better organize the many major life demands that have been identified, the adult domains have been broken down into subdomains as indicated below:

EMPLOYMENT/EDUCATION
- General Job Skills
- General Education/Training Considerations
- Employment Setting
- Career Refinement and Re-evaluation

HOME AND FAMILY
- Home Management
- Financial Management
- Family Life
- Child Rearing

LEISURE PURSUITS
- Indoor Activities
- Outdoor Activities
- Community/Neighborhood Activities
- Travel
- Entertainment

COMMUNITY INVOLVEMENT
- Citizenship
- Community Awareness
- Services/Resources

PHYSICAL/EMOTIONAL HEALTH
- Physical Health
- Emotional Health

PERSONAL RESPONSIBILITY AND RELATIONSHIPS
- Personal Confidence/Understanding
- Goal Setting
- Self-Improvement
- Relationships
- Personal Expression

These subdomains will be used in the next section, and they provide the organizational structure for the list of commercially available life skills materials found in Appendix A.

With a top-down perspective of curriculum development, it is useful to begin with general dimensions for organizing the events and activities associated with adulthood. However, perhaps the most important component of the model shown in Figure 2.1 is the identification of the major life demands. The next section of this chapter provides our list of these demands and a process for identifying the specific life skills needed to handle them.

MAJOR LIFE DEMANDS

After studying the conceptualization of adult domains and recognizing the areas of adult functioning, one needs to consider the method by which children and adolescents will be prepared for those domains. Several approaches have been tried to develop curricula to teach students. The one chosen most often bases its objectives on content or textbooks, or from a developmental perspective. The framework of the curriculum development model offered in this guide is outcome-based or top-down driven.

Top-Down Process

The top-down process to curricular development is a powerful approach in determining the content being taught in today's schools. The top-down process, also referred to as the outcome-based approach (Champlin, 1991; Friedland, 1992; King & Evans, 1991; Spady, 1986; Spady & Marshall, 1991), identifies the objectives or competencies based on a student's desired outcomes. The top-down process is used extensively in many fields, for example: vocational technical programs, NASA training for space flight, and professional degree programs (e.g., doctors, lawyers, teachers, nurses). The question asked when developing a top-down curriculum in any area is "What are the competencies these individuals need to know in order to competently perform the adult tasks?" The outcomes of each job are examined first to provide the foundation for building the curriculum. Outcomes are examined to determine the competencies needed to perform the tasks of the job. Those identified competencies or objectives are then organized into a curriculum or program of study. If any of the aforementioned fields and occupations did not develop curriculum from the top down, many of our professionals would be haphazardly trained. The need to utilize a top-down approach for any adult outcome-oriented curriculum is imperative, even more so in teaching all students with special needs for the basic everyday demands of adulthood.

Conceptual basis of top-down development for life skills curriculum development. The generation of a life skills curriculum developed from the top-down process needs to begin at the local level. Local needs should drive the focus of the competencies of the curriculum. There are "generic" or general competencies or life demands that all adults face, such as transportation, shopping, banking, and driving, which should be addressed in every life skills curriculum. The local generation of life skill competencies in the curriculum will reflect the differences in many locales throughout the United States—urban/rural, small community/ big city, regional, and sometimes even within states. The differences reflected in locally generated curricula include vocabulary (such as use of the word "neutral ground" for median on a street or boulevard), transportation (subway, ferry, bus, streetcar, etc.), culture (type of music, such as country, pop, soul, jazz), shopping practices (bagging versus not bagging your own groceries), and driving ordinances (right turn on red, U-turns, etc.). The identification of specific life skills by local school personnel when developing a life skills curriculum must reflect the competencies needed to be successful in that particular community.

Identification of Major Life Demands

The identification of curricular content in a life skills curriculum should be based on the behaviors that individuals will need in their specific community environments. The major domains of adult functioning, identified earlier in this chapter, provide the format or structure from which to identify workable classifications called subdomains to generate the major life demands. The subdomains organize the adult domains into workable categories for long-range goal planning. The major life demands provide the foundation for local school systems

to generate/develop/identify life skills for competency/course development.

The identification of the major life demands for this guide drew upon the combined experiences of the authors' teaching experiences, school-based personnel, and other professionals interested in life skill instruction, personal schooling, consultation with colleagues, study of relevant literature, observation of students, parents, teachers, siblings, friends, and strangers. This listing of major life demands is provided in Table 2.2 and represents a core from which life skills curricula, competencies, instructional objectives, courses, and activities can emerge. Additional life demands, created by school-based personnel, should reflect those demands and tasks deemed necessary in the specific community in which the students live and, therefore, need to know in order to function successfully in that environment. These community- or individual-specific life demands are necessary in order to realize the most complete and efficient transition programs for each student during their years in secondary programs at the junior and senior high levels. This will be discussed in detail in chapter 5, "Programming for Adult Outcomes."

Table 2.2 lists the six adult domains, 23 subdomains, and 147 major life demands. The major life demands represent the events or activities typically encountered by most adults in everyday life. It is from these demands that specific life skills, or the competencies needed to perform major life demands, will be generated to develop instructional objectives for the student's Individualized Education Program (IEP)/Individual Transition Plan (ITP).

TABLE 2.2. Major Life Demands

Domain	*Subdomain*	*Life Demands*
EMPLOYMENT/ EDUCATION	*General Job Skills*	seeking and securing a job learning job skills maintaining one's job understanding fundamental and legal issues
	General Education/ Training Considerations	knowing about education/training options gaining entry to post-secondary education/training settings (higher education, adult education, community education, trade/technical schools, military service) finding financial support utilizing academic and system survival skills (e.g., study skills, organizational skills, and time management) requesting employment services when needed (e.g., VR, unemployment) accessing support services of training setting
	Employment Setting	recognizing job duties and responsibilities exhibiting appropriate work habits/behavior getting along with employer and co-workers understanding company policies (e.g., fringe benefits, wages, sick/personal leave, advancement procedures) understanding take-home pay/deductions managing employment-related expenses (travel, clothes, dues) understanding OSHA regulations
	Career Refinement and Re-evaluation	revitalizing career choice exploring alternative career options pursuing career change
HOME AND FAMILY	*Home Management*	setting up household operations (e.g., initiating utilities) arranging furniture and equipment identifying and implementing security provisions and safety procedures cleaning dwelling maintaining and landscaping a yard laundering and maintaining clothes and household items performing/contracting for home repairs/improvements and regular maintenance storing household items maintaining automobile(s) and equipment, appliances, etc. reacting to environmental dangers (e.g., pollution, extreme weather conditions)
	Financial Management	creating a general financial plan (e.g., savings, investments, retirement) maintaining a budget using banking services paying bills establishing a good credit rating purchasing day-to-day items (clothes, food, etc.) renting an apartment selecting and buying a house (building new/purchasing existing) making major purchases (e.g., auto) determining payment options for major purchases (cash, credit, layaway, debit card, finance plan, etc.) preparing and paying taxes

(Table continues)

TABLE 2.2. *Continued*

Domain	Subdomain	Life Demands
HOME AND FAMILY *(cont.)*	*Financial Management (cont.)*	buying insurance purchasing specialty items throughout the year (e.g., birthday gifts, Christmas gifts, etc.) planning for long-term financial needs (e.g., major purchases, children's education) obtaining government assistance when needed (e.g., Medicare, food stamps, student loans)
	Family Life	preparing for marriage, family maintaining physical/emotional health of family members maintaining family harmony scheduling and managing daily, weekly, monthly, yearly family events (e.g., appointments, social events, leisure/recreational pursuits) planning and preparing meals (menu, buying food, ordering take-out food, dining out) arranging for/providing day care (children or older relatives) managing incoming/outgoing mail
	Child Rearing	acquiring realistic information about raising children preparing for pregnancy & childbirth understanding childhood development (physical, emotional, cognitive, language) managing children's behavior preparing for out-of-home experiences (e.g., day care, school) helping children with school-related needs hiring and training in-home babysitter
LEISURE PURSUITS	*Indoor Activities*	playing table/electronic games (e.g., cards, board games, puzzles, Nintendo, arcades, etc.) performing individual physical activities (e.g., weight training, aerobics, dance, swimming, martial arts) participating in group physical activities (e.g., racquetball, basketball) engaging in individual hobbies and crafts (e.g., reading, handicrafts, sewing, collecting)
	Outdoor Activities	performing individual physical activities (e.g., jogging, golf, bicycling, swimming, hiking, backpacking, fishing) participating in group physical activities (e.g., softball, football, basketball, tennis) engaging in general recreational activities (e.g., camping, sightseeing, picnicking)
	Community/ Neighborhood Activities	going to various ongoing neighborhood events (e.g., garage sales, block parties, BBQs) attending special events (e.g., fairs, trade shows, carnivals, parades, festivals)
	Travel	preparing to go on a trip (e.g., destination, transportation arrangements, hotel/motel arrangements, packing, preparations for leaving home) dealing with the realities of travel via air, ground, or water
	Entertainment	engaging in in-home activities (e.g., TV, videos, music) attending out-of-home events (e.g., theaters, spectator sports, concerts, performances, art shows) going to socially oriented events (e.g., restaurants, parties, nightclubs) and other social events

(Table continues)

TABLE 2.2. *Continued*

Domain	Subdomain	Life Demands
COMMUNITY INVOLVEMENT	*Citizenship*	understanding legal rights exhibiting civic responsibility voting in elections understanding tax obligations obeying laws and ordinances serving on a jury understanding judicial procedures (e.g., due process, criminal/civil courts, legal documents) attending public hearings creating change in the community (e.g., petition drives)
	Community Awareness	being aware of social issues affecting community knowing major events at the local, regional, national, world levels using mass media (TV, radio, newspaper) understanding all sides of public opinion on community issues recognizing and acting on fraudulent practices
	Services/ Resources	knowing about the wide range of services available in a specific community using all levels of government agencies (tax office, drivers licence [DMV], permits, consumer agencies [BBB]) accessing public transportation (trains, buses, subways, ferries, etc.) accessing private services (humane society, cable services, utilities [phone, water, electric, sewage, garbage]) accessing emergency services/resources (police, EMS, hospital, fire, civil defense) accessing agencies that provide special services (advocacy centers) securing legal representation (e.g., lawyer reference service)
PHYSICAL/ EMOTIONAL HEALTH	*Physical*	living a healthy lifestyle planning a nutritional diet exercising regularly as part of lifestyle having regular physical/dental checkups understanding illnesses and medical/dental needs across age levels using proper dental hygiene/dental care preventing illness and accidents recognizing health risks recognizing signs of medical/dental problems reacting to medical emergencies administering simple first aid using medications providing treatment for chronic health problems recognizing and accommodating physical changes associated with aging recognizing and dealing with substance use/abuse
	Emotional	understanding emotional needs across age levels recognizing signs of emotional needs managing life changes managing stress dealing with adversity and depression dealing with anxiety coping with separation/death of family members and friends understanding emotional dimensions of sexuality seeking personal counseling

(Table continues)

TABLE 2.2. *Continued*

Domain	Subdomain	Life Demands
PERSONAL RESPONSIBILITY AND RELATIONSHIPS	*Personal Confidence/ Understanding*	recognizing one's strengths and weaknesses appreciating one's accomplishments identifying ways to maintain or achieve a positive self-concept reacting appropriately to the positive or negative feedback of others using appropriate communication skills following one's religious beliefs
	Goal Setting	evaluating one's values identifying and achieving personal goals and aspirations exercising problem-solving/decision-making skills becoming independent and self-directed
	Self-Improvement	pursuing personal interests conducting self-evaluation seeking continuing education improving scholastic abilities displaying appropriate personal interaction skills maintaining personal appearance
	Relationships	getting along with others establishing and maintaining friendships developing intimate relations deciding upon potential spouse or partner being sensitive to the needs of others communicating praise or criticism to others being socially perceptive (e.g., recognizing contextual clues) dealing with conflict nurturing healthy child/parent interactions solving marital problems
	Personal Expression	sharing personal feelings, experiences, concerns, desires with other people writing personal correspondence (e.g., letters, notes, greeting cards)

EXAMPLES OF SPECIFIC LIFE SKILLS IDENTIFICATION

This section provides an example from each of the adult domains previously discussed. Figure 2.3 illustrates the actual sequence suggested for identifying specific life skills for an example from the Employment/Education domain. Table 2.3 contains information related to the other five domains that could be put into the sequence displayed in Figure 2.3. It is important to note that these examples only provide a sampling of possible specific life skills that are associated with a given major life demand. The listed skills are by no means exhaustive of the life skills competence necessary for dealing with the selected major life demands.

In Figure 2.3, Employment/Education—Seeking and Securing a Job, is one example of a major life demand from which several specific life skills are generated. The adult domain called Employment/ Education has four subdomains (General Job Skills, Employment Setting Considerations, Education/ Training, and Career Refinement and Re-evaluation). The life demand "seeking and securing a job" can be found under the first subdomain, General Job Skills. This particular major life demand can be associated with several life skills.

Process	*EXAMPLE*
# ADULT DOMAINS	EMPLOYMENT/EDUCATION HOME AND FAMILY LEISURE PURSUITS COMMUNITY INVOLVEMENT EMOTIONAL/PHYSICAL HEALTH PERSONAL RESPONSIBILITIES AND RELATIONSHIPS
## SUBDOMAIN	GENERAL JOB SKILLS EMPLOYMENT SETTING CONSIDERATIONS EDUCATION/TRAINING CAREER REFINEMENT AND RE-EVALUATION
Major Life Demand	• Seeking and Securing a Job
Specific Life Skills	• identifying marketable job skills and interests • identifying sources of job possibilities • using all sources of available jobs to identify appropriate jobs for the skills you possess • sending letters of inquiry or making calls of inquiry regarding the job, its availability, and application procedures • locating the site of the prospective job on the map • determining transportation needs for prospective jobs • obtaining and filling out a job application • calling for an interview appointment • recording time, place, location, and name of person interviewing for future reference • determining appropriate dress for interview • practicing interview skills • generating list of questions to ask about the job • computing weekly or monthly income • calculating mileage to work • asking about subsequent evaluations of job performance • identifying appropriate dress for the job

Figure 2.3. Sequence for Identifying Specific Life Skills.

TABLE 2.3. Examples of Specific Life Skills Identification

Adult Domain	Specific Subdomain	Major Life Demand	Specific Life Skills
Employment and Education	General Job Skills	Seeking and securing a job	[see Figure 2.3]
Home and Family	Financial Management	Purchasing day-to-day items (e.g., clothes)	• know where to shop • compare prices • understand cleaning/care instructions • aware of available money in checking account
Leisure Pursuits	Entertainment	Engaging in in-home activities (e.g., renting videos)	• compare prices at various video stores • determine costs and amount of available cash • identify video store and location • understand terms of video rental • agree on movie selection with others • know how to use VCR
Community Involvement	Citizenship	Voting in elections	• register to vote • identify appropriate polling place and its location • obtain information on offices and candidates • determine distance from home to polling place • schedule time to vote
Physical and Emotional Health	Physical	Recognize signs of medical/dental problems	• know symptoms of common illnesses (e.g., flu) • determine the temperature of your body • know when to call or go to the doctor • describe symptoms over the phone to health care worker • understand the roles of doctor, nurse, pharmacist
Personal Responsibility and Interpersonal Relationships	Self-Improvement	Maintaining personal appearance	• buy appropriate clothes for work • understand directions for cleaning work clothes • wear appropriate clothes for weather • style hair when needed • brush/floss teeth regularly

The generation of the life skills, as mentioned earlier in this section, depends on local needs and expectations for success in each community. The importance of this local input cannot be overstated. The success of programs is reflected in the ability of students performing adult tasks within their own community. Curriculum development in the schools must reflect those adult tasks.

This chapter discussed the identification of major life demands and specific life skills. The importance of the top-down process in developing curriculum cannot be overstated. This outcome-based approach endorsed by many educators will help ensure success and improvement of quality of life for all students.

Integrating Life Skills Content Into the Curriculum

The identification of major life demands and the specific life skills that accompany them is a major component of the top-down model of curriculum development. However, unless this information is translated into practice, all is for naught. The next critical step in the model (Figure 2.1) after the generation of major life demands requires individuals involved in curriculum development or, more precisely, those responsible for what is actually taught to students, to integrate life skills topics and instruction into the curricular structure within which they must operate.

The case has already been made for the importance of covering life skills content before students exit from formal schooling. Now the case must be made that it is possible to do this regardless of the educational environment in which students are placed. This chapter provides suggestions for teaching life skills whether the students are fully included in regular education or receive their education in less-integrated settings.

EDUCATIONAL PLACEMENTS OF STUDENTS WITH DISABILITIES

The *Fourteenth Annual Report to Congress on the Implementation of the Individuals with Disabilities Education Act* (U.S. Department of Education, 1992) paints a varied scenario of education placement of students with disabilities. Statistically, where students are placed to receive special education services varies greatly across states. Aggregate data on placement—this includes 50 states, District of Columbia, and territories—for the higher-incidence disability categories as well as all disabilities combined are presented in Table 3.1. Figures represent the percentage of students (ages 6–21) from a specific categorical group who are placed in the three most common settings: regular class, resource room, or separate class.

Table 3.1 shows significant variability across categorical groups as well. Examining the extent of time that students spend in regular education settings (the categories labeled "regular education" and "resource room"), some interesting differences become obvious. The majority of students with learning disabilities (77%) are receiving most of their education in regular education settings—combining the regular education and resource figures, while very few students who have been identified as mentally retarded (27%) find themselves in similar arrangements. Not surprisingly, less than half of those students designated as having emotional problems (43%) spend the better part of their educational day in regular education environments.

The logistical implications of these data for teaching life skills to such students suggest that

TABLE 3.1. Percentage of Students Age 6–21 Served in Different Educational Environments During 1989–90 School Year

Environment	All Disabilities	Learning Disabilities	Serious Emotional Disturbance	Mental Retardation
Regular Class	31.5%	20.7%	14.9%	6.7%
Resource Room	37.6%	56.1%	28.5%	20.1%
Separate Class	24.8%	21.7%	37.1%	61.1%

Source. U.S. Department of Education. (1992). *Fourteenth annual report to Congress on the implementation of the Individuals with Disabilities Education Act.* Washington, DC: Office of Special Education Programs, Office of Special Education and Rehabilitative Services.

options for delivering instruction are needed. For students who spend all of their instructional day in regular education and receive consultant services from special education personnel, life skills topics have to be worked into the established curriculum. While this previous suggestion holds for students receiving resource services when they are in regular education settings, special education teachers can infuse life skills topics into the designated content they must cover with these students when they are in the resource room. They can also augment prescribed instruction with additional life skills topics that may be related but are separate from what they must cover.

For students who are in special education settings for at least the greater part of their instructional day, other more comprehensive options such as life skills coursework may be viable. The other options described above—infusion and augmentation—are also possible. Overriding issues such as credit versus noncredit courses or the particular philosophy of a school (i.e., school-based decision making) or school district may dictate the nature of certain programs.

OPTIONS FOR ORGANIZING LIFE SKILLS CONTENT FOR INSTRUCTION

A realistic appraisal of the adult outcome needs of students, the current educational placements of students, and various school restructuring movements

suggests that a continuum of options for delivering life skills instruction is warranted. Such a continuum is represented graphically in Figure 3.1. The continuum represents variations in the amount of time available for covering life skills topics. The option at the bottom of the continuum implies that the nature of the curriculum is life skills oriented. The option at the top of the continuum represents a scenario in which content other than life skills is emphasized. In between these two extremes are other viable options depending circumstances.

One should not necessarily conclude that the continuum completely reflects the distinction between inclusive educational settings and segregated placements. It is very possible that a diploma-generating regular education program might be life skills oriented or that the infusion approach may have to be implemented in a pullout vocational program that does not cover essential life skills.

The important message is that teaching life skills to students with special needs is needed and that it can be done to some extent regardless of the educational environment in which the students are placed. This is not to say that substantial and sometimes impenetrable barriers prevent such instruction from occurring.

The remainder of this section provides examples of how the various options highlighted in Figure 3.1 can be implemented. We have arbitrarily categorized the continuum into three types of approaches for integrating life skills content into the curriculum: infusion approach, augmentation approach, and coursework approach. Table 3.2 summarizes the different options presented in the following discussion.

CONTINUUM OF LIFE SKILLS

Infusion of
Life Skills Topics
Into Established
Content of
Existing Course(s)

Portion of
Existing Course(s)
Dedicated to
Life Skills Topics

Single Generic
Life Skills
Course

Select
Topical
Life Skills
Course(s)

Comprehensive
Grouping of
Specific
Life Skills
Courses

Figure 3.1. Options for Integrating Life Skills Content into the Curriculum.

Infusion Approach

Rationale. This approach is used when students are in a curricular orientation that is tightly regimented and allows neither for elective coursework nor the allocation of time to cover additional topics. Frequently it will apply to the situation in which students are fully included in regular education classes and, if they are on the secondary level, are likely to be in diploma-track programs.

Procedure for implementing. Two requirements are needed for teachers to infuse life skills instruction into existing course content. First, teachers need to be familiar with various major life demands and resulting specific life skills such as those presented in chapter 2. Second, teachers must be aware of the specific topics presented in the instructional materials being used. It is critical to capitalize on the teachable moments created by existing content. Once a topic is identified as having life skill relevance, attention must be directed to it and then coverage can ensue.

Ideally, teachers (especially special-education teachers providing consultant services to regular-education teachers) would preview materials to identify all the topics that could be expanded into a discussion of functional value. Once these topics are identified, some preparation for covering them from a life skills perspective may be needed. If done with enough lead time, teachers could obtain materials that may serve as resources for the discussion. Appendix A of this guide can be used for this purpose. It seems that special education teachers will find that having knowledge about life skills and how to make existing content more relevant to students is a valuable asset in their work with regular-education teachers.

The major drawback to the infusion approach is that the life skills addressed are dictated by the topics in the instructional materials. This approach certainly leads to an incomplete coverage of the many life demands for which students need to be prepared. However, this approach offers some attractive benefits for students and teachers: At least students are taught some life skills, and infusing life skills topics into the existing curriculum will make instruction more meaningful to students. A secondary outcome is that students are likely to be more excited about the topics being presented.

TABLE 3.2. Comparison of Various Options for Teaching Life Skills Content

Curricular Option	Nature of Curricular Approach	Appropriateness for		Appropriateness for		Curricular Example
		Regular Education	Special Education	Elementary Level	Secondary Level	
Infusion into existing content	infusion	Y	Y	Y	Y	Working in a discussion of how to treat athlete's foot when the topic of fungus is covered in a general science textbook
Dedicated portion of course	augmentation	Y	Y	Y	Y	Unit on "the financial implications of dating" in addition to the regular content of a "consumer math" course
Generic Life Skills Course	distinct course	(Y)	Y	N	Y	Course entitled "Life 101"
Topical Life Skills Course	distinct course	(Y)	Y	N	Y	Course entitled "Math in the Real World"
Comprehensive Arrangement of Life Skills Courses	distinct set of courses	Y/N	Y	N	Y	Set of courses such as: Personal Finance, Practical Math, Health and Hygiene, Everyday Science, Practical Communications, Community Awareness and Involvement, Occupational Development, Interpersonal Relations

Examples. Because this option may become even more viable in the next few years, we are providing four examples of how this infusion technique could be used. A similar format will be used in presenting each of the examples. First, the title of the course will be given, with an indication of whether the course is credit or noncredit; second, the specific topic being covered in the course will be highlighted; third, selected life skills activities/topics that could be chosen to infuse into the topic, along with any appropriate major life demands (Figure 2.2), are offered.

1. **Course:** Consumer Math Course (credit)

    Topic Being Covered: "Keeping Basic Financial Records"

    Life Skills Activities To Be Infused [Major Life Demand]:
    • Discuss record-keeping systems needed for managing family finances. [Maintaining a budget, preparing and paying taxes]
    • Examine occupations that require financial record-keeping skills. [Seeking and securing a job]
    • Examine various types of community involvement that involve financial record-keeping skills. [Creating change in the community (e.g., volunteer work on a community fundraiser)]

2. **Course:** United States History (credit)

    Topic Being Covered: "Women's Rights"

    Life Skills Activities To Be Infused [Major Life Demand]:
    • Discuss the topic of discrimination. [Being sensitive to the needs of others]
    • Identify the procedures to register to vote. [Using all levels of government agencies]

- Discuss the issues and candidates' positions of an upcoming election. [Knowing major events at the local, regional, national, and international levels]
- Write to the League of Women Voters to share concern. [Sharing personal feelings, experience, concerns, and desires with other people]

3. **Course:** General Science (credit)

   Topic Being Covered: "Fungus" in a section entitled "All Living Things Are Made of Cells"

   Life Skills Activities To Be Infused [Major Life Demand]:

   - Discuss how one can contract, treat, and prevent athlete's foot. [Understanding illnesses and medical/dental needs across age levels]

4. **Course:** Environmental Science (noncredit)

   Topic Being Covered: "Ecosystems"

   Life Skills Activities To Be Infused [Major Life Demand]:

   - Discuss the balance needed in a salt water aquarium. [Engaging in individual hobbies and crafts]
   - Discuss environmental issues of local concern. [Understanding all sides of public opinion on community issues]

These examples are presented to give a taste of what can be done to make content life skills relevant.

Augmentation Approach

Rationale. This option can be used in those situations where there is some time available to cover additional topics—other than those prescribed by course description. In reality most courses probably fall into this category in that the teacher has some degree of discretion regarding topics covered. This option allows the integration of life skills topics that usually relate to a similar topic being covered in the course.

In some cases, one class period each week may be specifically dedicated to covering life skills; in other situations, life skills will be covered when there is relevance to course content. The distinguishing feature between this option and the previous one is that a greater portion of allocated course time is dedicated to covering life skills.

Procedures. What teachers need to do is quite simple: identify life skills areas, develop or identify a unit on the topic, plan for teaching the unit, and deliver the instruction. Again, familiarity with the major demands of adulthood may be helpful. The same attractive and limiting features described for the infusion approach apply to this approach. One difference, however, is that more teacher preparation time may be needed in an augmentation approach, since more class time is being devoted to this instruction.

Examples. All of the scenarios used to exemplify the infusion approach could be used here as well. Where cursory attention is given to the life skills topics in an infusion approach, more in-depth coverage is given to such topics in an augmentation approach.

For instance, for the topic of "Women's Rights," an entire unit on discrimination "then and now" could be presented. Such a unit could provide extensive coverage of this topic and would be of great value to students with special needs—some of whom may know very well the personal insult that accompanies discriminatory practices. The athlete's foot topic could be expanded into a fascinating unit on preventing health problems.

Another example that shows how a topic could be augmented to cover real-world needs is to spend some time on the "economics of dating" when teaching a course on consumer mathematics. Few topics spark more interest and enthusiasm in adolescents than this one, as it has real meaning to most of them. An intriguing unit could be developed that would examine the costs of going out on a date. Activities could be planned to have students decide with whom they would want to go, where they want to go, what they want to do, what they think it will cost, and ultimately, what is does cost to go on this date. The outcomes of such a unit reinforce the principles presented in the consumer math course and assuredly teach some important life skills.

Coursework Approach

Rationale. This approach is used when the curriculum allows for the development of separate courses. There are a number of variations related to this option, from developing one generic life skills course that covers many different topical areas to a set of different topical life skills courses. The advantage of the coursework option is that more time can be devoted to functional content, and it can be organized according to adult needs rather than being dictated by other course content.

Although the common interpretation is that life skills coursework does not generate credit toward graduation, this does not have to be the case. It is possible to develop coursework with a functional focus that meets all of the requirements of a credit course. For that matter, an alternative curriculum could be developed composed entirely of life skills coursework that would cover the areas of math, science, social studies, and language arts/English. One such effort adapted an adult education program, Adult Performance Level (APL) Project, for use with special populations of students. The authors of the adaptation project designed it so that all of the coursework could be credit generating (LaQuey, 1981).

Procedures. Not unlike the previously discussed options, the development of coursework should be based on the future needs of students. A recommended procedure for the development of the content to be covered in life skills courses, presented in Figure 3.2, is discussed below. (We recognize that other administrative requirements may be necessary; they will be addressed in chapter 6.)

1. *Decide on the major goals for the course in terms of both content and instruction.* What outcomes are students to demonstrate? How is instruction going to be delivered and content covered (i.e., textbooks, community-based)?

2. *Develop a scope and sequence to the content to be covered.* This should be based on students' current and future needs, as determined by a realistic appraisal of probable subsequent environments. Identification of potential topics for inclusion in coursework might involve selecting topics from existing resources such as the list of major life demands contained in Table 2.2 of this guide or the

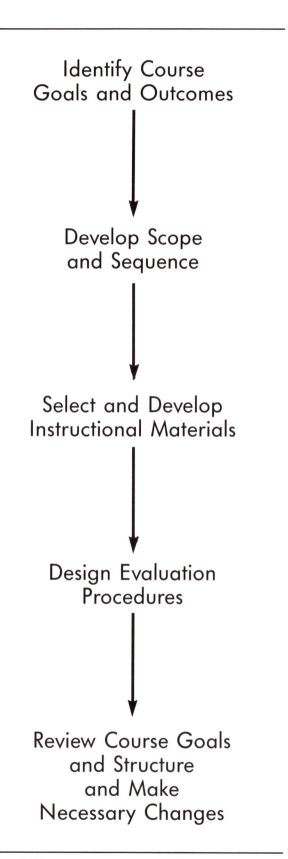

Figure 3.2. Course Development Process.

listing of competencies/subcompetencies from other sources such as Brolin's (1991) *Life-Centered Career Education* program.

3. *Select instructional materials that will be helpful in accomplishing the goals of the course.* (Appendix A of this guide should be helpful with this task.) It is possible that teachers want to use a textbook in certain courses. We recommend using systematic techniques for selecting these types of materials. Some school systems have implemented excellent ways of maintaining overall course goals when selecting textbooks for life skills courses (L. Helmke, personal communication, April 28, 1992). It may be necessary to develop one's own or solicit materials from community sources, since there may not be any commercial ones available. Ways of dealing with this problem are discussed in the next chapter.

4. *Design a procedure to evaluate the effectiveness of the life skills coursework.* It is extremely important to create mechanisms for assessing how well life skills are being taught and how well students are learning them. The social validity of any course rests in how well the content covered benefits the students either immediately or at some later point. As a result, it might be necessary to conduct follow-up studies of students to determine if the life skills taught are indeed important in their lives and whether they show competence in performing them.

5. *Review course goals and structure and make changes as necessary.* All programs should be considered temporary offerings. Curricular change and innovation should be a scheduled part of all programs. It will be essential to revise life skills courses to adapt to an ever-changing world.

Examples. As suggested in Figure 3.1, there are three listed options that involve the coursework option: a single generic life skills course; selected topical life skills courses; or a comprehensive grouping of specific life skills courses.

A single generic course might be called something like "Life 101." It would include topics from all of the major adult domains (Figure 2.2). It is also likely to address content that cuts across the typical subject area distinctions of science, social studies, math, and English/language arts. If this course is developed properly, it not only would be extremely valuable to students with special needs, but it could also appeal to all students in a school, possibly as an elective course.

A topical life skills course could take one of two different forms. One format is a course designed entirely around an adult domain. For instance, and entire course could easily address the topic of home and family. In many schools, courses along these lines do exist and should be considered for inclusion in a student's program of studies. The second format focuses on a more traditional area. An example of a math course along these lines is "Math in the Real World"—a course designed to cover math that has real-world relevance. Some of the possible topics that could be part of this course are presented in Figure 3.3.

The last option relates to the situation where a series of life skills courses is offered. This will usually occur in schools that provide innovative alternative functional curricula that generate credit toward graduation or functional curricula for students who are not in diploma track programs. While the first scenario is very possible, the second one is more likely to be the case.

A suggested series of life skills coursework is presented under this option in Table 3.2. The organizational scheme for the development of these courses is an attempt to cover the areas of math, science, social studies, and communication. Each course includes coverage of the major life demands we all must face. Selected examples of some of the content from each of the courses are provided in Table 3.3.

It is critical to understand that all of these courses involve the use of important scholastic and social skills in functional contexts. The next section shows how life skills relate to the scholastic and social skills typically associated with mastery of the school curriculum and equated with competence.

Living within one's means

Estimating   Profit and loss

Areas, surfaces, and volumes

Percentages   Hire and purchase

Signed numbers   Taxes

Interest   Tables and graphics

Ratio and proportion   Geometry

Travel and transportation

Games and chance

Math for
home maintenance and repair

Figure 3.3. Math in the Real World.

RELATIONSHIP OF SCHOLASTIC AND SOCIAL SKILLS TO LIFE SKILLS

Understanding the relationship of scholastic and social skills to acquisition of life skills is important. One must comprehend the concerns and fears of significant individuals (parents, administrators, teachers) that each exiting student should master basic competencies before leaving the school system.

Importance of the Relationship

Every community leader, parent, school board member, administrator, and teacher is concerned about students' ability to read, write, listen, speak, solve problems, and use math concepts. The concern also extends to the students' ability to survive in different situations and environments and get along with those they meet. The acquisition of these skills is paramount to students' success on the job and as a community member. As teachers, we work hard to see that these skills are instilled in every student prior to their exit from formal schooling.

In addition to concern about students' acquiring basic academic, social, and survival skills, community leaders, parents, school board members, administrators, and teachers also hope that each student will leave the formal school experience with the skills to be successful as an adult in the community. Life skills instruction fulfills that role.

The merging of basic skills instruction and life skills instruction for adult outcome-based programs provides a likely solution to the critical concerns of all. Figures 3.4 and 3.5 outline examples of how the integration of these concepts into students' programs can take place.

Selected Examples Across School Levels

Figures 3.4 and 3.5 present sample activities that incorporate basic skills with the adult domains (under which major life demands and life skills are identified). These matrices exemplify the application of basic academic skills and social and survival skills to everyday adult tasks or life skills. The activities illustrate these functional applications.

Activities emphasizing functional application of basic skills can be found at any grade level. Figure 3.4, the Elementary Matrix, outlines examples of activities that are appropriate at the elementary level. These examples highlight the relatively simplistic types of tasks that are, in many cases, preliminary to other activities which students are expected to master later in their programs. In many cases the activities are introductory to a concept that will be mastered in a couple of years.

Figure 3.5, the Secondary Matrix, illustrates activities that would more commonly be associated with older students who are a few months to a few years from exiting the program. These tasks represent a level of performance that is expected of any successful adult in the community. These

TABLE 3.3. Life Skills Courses and Select Sample Topics

Life Skills Course	Select Topics
Personal Finance	maintaining a budget filing tax submitting an application for a loan using credit cards
Practical Math	performing home repairs/maintenance estimating travel time cooking measuring dosage of prescribed medicine
Health & Hygiene	dealing with illness administering first aid maintaining one's personal appearance handling stress
Everyday Science	gardening identifying how things work controlling pests using science in the kitchen
Practical Communication	using resource materials requesting information writing personal cards and notes taking phone messages
Community Awareness and Involvement	registering to vote using community resources (e.g., library) attending neighborhood association meetings knowing one's legal rights
Occupational Development	identifying personal interests and aptitudes preparing a career planning packet practicing interview skills identifying available jobs in the community
Interpersonal Relations	getting along with others accepting criticism complimenting others engaging in social conversation

Graphics by Lori Kopp.

	Employment/ Education	Home and Family	Leisure Pursuits	Community Involvement	Emotional/ Physical Health	Personal Responsibility/ Relationships
Reading	Read library books on various occupations	Read directions to prepare brownies from a mix	Look for ads in the newspaper for toys	Read road signs and understand what they mean	Locate poison control numbers in the phone book	Read a story to a younger child
Writing	Write to the school board about a pothole in the school driveway	Make a list of items needed from the grocery store	Fill out a magazine order form completely	Complete an application to play little league	Keep a daily diary of food you eat in each food group	Write a thank-you note to a relative for a gift
Listening	Listen to a lecture by a bank official on savings accounts	Listen to a lecture on babysitting tips	Listen to radio/TV to see if a ball game is rained out	Listen to a lecture on how children can recycle	Listen to the school nurse explain the annual eye exam for your class	Listen to a friend describe their family vacation
Speaking	Discuss reasons we work	Ask parents for permission to stay at a friend's house	Invite friends over to play Monopoly	Discuss park and playground improvements with the mayor	Ask the school nurse how to care for mosquito bites	Discuss honesty, trust, and promise. Define them.
Math Applications	Calculate how much you would make babysitting at $1.25 an hour for 3 hours	Compute the cost of a box of cereal using a coupon	Compute the cost of going to the movies	Compute tax on a video game	Calculate and compare the cost of different types of Band-Aids. Include tax.	Ask a friend to share a candy bar. Calculate your part of the cost.
Problem-Solving	Decide which environment you work best in: out or in; quiet or noisy; active or at a desk, etc.	Decide how to share TV time with a sibling	Given $15 for the afternoon which would you do: go to the movies, go bowling, or play videos?	Role-play the times you would use the 911 emergency number	Decide how many hours of sleep you need per night	Decide if you have enough coins to purchase a vending-machine soda for you and your friend
Survival Skills	Keep homework assignments in a special notebook	Develop a checklist of what to do before and after school	Use a map to find the best way to the mall	Draw a map of the way they go to/from school	Mark the calendar for your next dental appointment	Identify important table manners
Personal/ Social	Ask a classmate to assist you with a job	Settle a dispute with a sibling	Call a video store to see if they have a specific movie	Role-play asking a police officer for help if you're lost	Ask a friend to go bicycling with you	Role-play appropriate behavior for various places (movies, church, restaurant, ballpark)

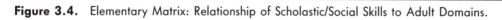

Figure 3.4. Elementary Matrix: Relationship of Scholastic/Social Skills to Adult Domains.

	Employment/ Education	Home and Family	Leisure Pursuits	Community Involvement	Emotional/ Physical Health	Personal Responsibility/ Relationships
Reading	reading classified ads for jobs	interpreting bills	locating and understanding movie information in a newspaper	following directions on tax forms	comprehending directions on medication	reading letters from friends
Writing	writing a letter of application for a job	writing checks	writing for information on a city to visit	filling in a voter registration form	filling in your medical history on forms	sending thank-you notes
Listening	understanding oral directions of a procedure change	comprehending oral directions about making dinner	listening for forecast to plan outdoor activity	understanding campaign ads	attending lectures on stress	taking turns in a conversation
Speaking	asking your boss for a raise	discussing morning routines with family	inquiring about tickets for a concert	stating your opinion at the school board meeting	describing symptoms to a doctor	giving feedback to a friend about the purchase of a compact disc
Math Applications	understanding difference between net and gross pay	computing the cost of doing laundry in a laundromat versus at home	calculating the cost of a dinner out versus eating at home	obtaining information for a building permit	using a thermometer	planning the costs of a date
Problem-Solving	settling a dispute with a co-worker	deciding how much to budget for rent	role-playing appropriate behaviors for various places	knowing what to do if you are the victim of fraud	selecting a doctor	deciding how to ask someone for a date
Survival Skills	using a prepared career planning packet	listing emergency phone numbers	using a shopping center directory	marking a calendar for important dates (e.g., recycling, garbage collection)	using a system to remember to take vitamins	developing a system to remember birthdays
Personal/ Social	applying appropriate interview skills	helping a child with homework	knowing the rules of a neighborhood pool	locating self-improvement classes	getting a yearly physical exam	discussing how to negotiate a price at a flea market

Figure 3.5. Secondary Matrix: Relationship of Scholastic/Social Skills to Adult Domains.

matrices provide teachers and others a working idea of the range of ability, age, and type of tasks that can be found in a life skills program. In addition, they offer an illustration of the relationship between needed basic skills and the real-life application of those skills to everyday situations.

This chapter provided suggestions for organizing and delivering life skills in varying academic or school situations. In addition, the relationship to teaching basic skills in solving real-life tasks at the elementary and secondary levels was discussed.

Instructional Considerations and Material Identification, Selection, and Development

In program development, certain instructional components can make the difference in successfully implementing a life skills curriculum. Considerations such as where the instruction takes place, the method or technique used, and the materials used during the instructional process are integral to student success in the program. This chapter will discuss instructional considerations and sources of materials as well as guidelines for selecting and creating materials.

INSTRUCTIONAL CONSIDERATIONS

Teachers need to consider best practices in teaching for adult outcomes when planning a life skills program in their classrooms. Edgar (1987, 1991), Mithaug, Horiuchi, and Fanning (1985), Murphy and Walsh (1989), and Neubert and Foster (1988) have suggested many factors that contribute to students' exiting from high school prepared for a successful adult experience. The literature overwhelmingly supports including the following in planning instruction for a life skills program. Those practices include teaching for the improvement of the student's quality of life, teaching adult outcome tasks, teaching those relevant adult tasks in the natural (community) environment, and teaching tasks related to

the students' probable subsequent experiences and environments. This section discusses the variables of classroom-based and community-based instruction.

Classroom-Based Instruction

Classroom instruction is important to prepare students for the basic elements of academics they will be applying in the natural environment. Practicing money identification, giving change, using calculators, decision making, and studying appropriate vocabulary for each life skill are examples of a few tasks that students can be introduced to and practice in the classroom.

Teachers can also prepare students by inviting resource people into the classroom. A resource person can be any individual who has experience and knowledge relevant to life skills being taught in the classroom. They can introduce concepts, describe their job or jobs associated with their business, outline the training needed to obtain a position similar to theirs, or share information on a specific topic (e.g., drug abuse, first aid). A list of resource people and organizations who provide speakers can be found in Appendix C (Potential Field Experience Sites and Speakers). In addition, Appendix D (Preparing for a Community Resource Person's Visit) provides several suggestions in preparing for visitors to the classroom.

Community-Based Instruction

One of the most important aspects of a life skills curriculum is the practicing or application of the life skills in the natural environment. This type of experience is very valuable for students. It builds their confidence and self-esteem to function in the community environment. We suggest that teachers start with on-campus experiences and move to community experiences when the students reach a level of success on campus.

On-campus experiences. Simple experiences around your school campus can be a good preparation experience for students prior to going into the community. Placing students with other teachers, the school secretary, cafeteria personnel, the librarian, custodians, the coach, or athletic director for a period of time every week (one hour, once a day, three times a week, etc.) will give both teachers and students a feel for their strengths and potential problems that might occur in the community.

Community experiences. Many times teachers, administrators, and parents are hesitant to extend teaching into the community environment. Much of this hesitation is due to past experiences they have had with field trips, the various negative connotations of these types of trips (e.g. fun, play, unstructured, no application to academics, etc.), transportation problems (e.g. no funds for school buses), and lack of understanding of the relationship of the field experience to the curriculum. We have found that a simple change of language better communicates the objective or goal of the excursion into the community. By changing the title from "field trip" to "field experience," teachers have found they have had more cooperation from students, parents, administrators, other teachers, and prospective field experience sites.

Teachers do not have difficulty finding field experience sites. Any place in the community is a potential site. Many teachers coordinate their visits to the community with life skill topics being studied by one or more students in their classes. The curriculum sets the pace and creates the need to visit the natural environment in which the life skill occurs in order to practice the skills learned or introduced in the classroom. A list of potential community field experiences is provided in Appendix C.

Experiences in the community involve a great deal of planning and coordination. Appendix E, Preparing for a Field Experience, outlines suggestions for teachers on preparing themselves, the students, and the individuals at the field experience site, as well as follow-up after the field experience.

Teachers who have ventured into the community realize the need for students to be evaluated on their experience. A simple evaluation instrument can be developed to evaluate students on any number of variables (e.g. social skills, how to make decisions, appropriate dress, use of academic skills or targeted life skills). Three samples of field experience checklists that have been field tested can be found in Appendix F.

MATERIAL IDENTIFICATION, SELECTION, AND DEVELOPMENT

The teacher's role in any life skills class will change as the teacher becomes integral in bringing real-life tasks, materials, and experiences to their students and in taking students into the community. Life skills content and information may not always come out of the traditional textbook but instead from items found in everyday life. Every teacher will concur that one of the most important and time-consuming jobs they have is reviewing, researching, ordering, preparing, making, and soliciting materials for instruction. Obtaining materials for a life skills program is no different. Organizing life skills materials involves resourcefulness, creativity, and, especially during the initial stages, a substantial amount of planning, start-up time, and effort.

Sources of Instructional Materials

Resources for life skills materials are as varied as the communities in which instruction occurs. Materials used for life skills instruction should reflect the subsequent environment in which the student will eventually function and use that skill. The type of material should also vary to provide motivation, stimulation, and variety to the students. When seeking materials for instructional purposes the teacher should consider each source equally. The following discussion outlines considerations for acquiring a variety of life skill materials for the classroom.

Those considerations include the correlation of each material with a real life task, the use and availability of commercially made materials, the use of teacher/student generated materials, the resources available in the community, and technology used in the community.

Real-life task correlation. As teachers consider materials for use in a life skills lesson, they need to reflect on the use of that material in real life. Is the material used in a real-life setting? Is it up-to-date, and does it reflects the best use for the student? Is this material a substitute for the real item? Is the real thing accessible to the student on site or do they have to go into the community to use it? Is it a realistic material for a particular student, taking into consideration their interests and ability levels? Ultimately teachers will want to use the real item in the natural environment if not the next best substitute for it.

Commercially available materials. In recent years, a deluge of commercially prepared materials has flooded the market. Many are addressing the problems that have for years plagued the typical materials used in high schools for students with special needs and those who are at risk. Problems such as low reading levels, lack of relevancy to student needs and interest, and "juvenile-looking" illustrations and concepts have been addressed by authors and publishers in currently available materials. Even though great strides have been made in the quality and appropriateness of the materials available for students, building a life skills library in a classroom can be time-consuming, difficult, and expensive.

The situation regarding acquisition of commercially available materials has gone from the problem of few commercially made materials available 10 years ago to too many in some life skill areas today. In addition, sorting through the available materials to determine reading level, content, cost, etc., is time consuming and, in some cases, impossible. Although each teacher should have the opportunity to review materials prior to purchasing them, this is rarely possible. In addition, teachers often do not even know what is available as they are not able to see catalogs (or have not received them), meet with publishing representatives, or attend conferences that have material exhibits. In addition, many teachers have very little, if any, money designated for them to spend on materials as they like. Limited budgets mean money must be spent wisely.

Having as much information about materials as possible beforehand makes material selection easier.

Appendix A provides a listing of many commercially available materials, although it is not designed to be a comprehensive list. This listing provides a general source for teachers on the availability of materials relating to the major life demands/subdomains identified in Table 2.2. A list of the publishers' addresses and phone numbers can be found in Appendix B. We suggest writing to or calling each company for a recent catalog to file for reference on current products and prices when money becomes available.

Each section of the Materials List in Appendix A corresponds to the subdomain(s) identified in Table 2.2. Column one contains the title of the material. The publisher's three-letter code is in column two. If they are stated in the publisher's catalog, the recommended age and reading level are listed in columns three and four, respectively. The type of the material (workbook, video, filmstrip, flash cards, etc.) can be found in column five. Figure 4.1 is an excerpt from the Materials List in Appendix A. This information should be useful in purchasing commercially produced materials.

Teacher/student generated materials. In some instances the materials needed for a particular lesson or task may not be commercially available. Teachers must then consider other alternatives. Creating the material is one option. A popular method of making teacher generated materials is using file folder lessons or topical instructional packets. The teacher can obtain cartons, labels from cans, applications, ads from newspapers and magazines, or any other items that have life skill relevancy from home or businesses in the community. The carton, label, or ad can then be glued on the outside of the folder or packet. Questions for students to answer can be written on note cards and stored in the folder itself. Students can write the answers on paper or do the activity orally with the instructor, paraprofessional, or peers in the class. The file folders or instructional packets can provide individualization for students who have specific needs or need additional work on specific life skills. In addition, these "homemade" materials are the perfect way to customize the materials and the curriculum to the local needs.

Many times teachers have a difficult time finding the extra hours to develop folders or instruc-

HOME MANAGEMENT

Material	Publisher	Age Level	Reading Level	Type
On My Own With Language	LSI	MS–HS	4.5–5.5	DM
Owning a Car	FJA	JH–HS	2.2–2.5	W
Paying With Promises	FJA	JH–HS	2.2–2.6	W
Peggy's Picture Cookbook	MEM	MS–HS	—	B

PUBLISHER

Publisher Code	Publisher Name
LSI	LinguiSystems
FJA	Fearon/Janus/Quercus
MEM	Media Materials, Inc.

TYPES OF MATERIALS

B	Book
DM	Duplicating Master
W	Workbook

AGE LEVELS

MS	Middle School
JH	Junior High School
HS	High School

Figure 4.1. Excerpt from Materials List.

tional packets. Calling upon students or assigning students to assist you in putting files or packets together not only involves them in the process but can also give them the opportunity to suggest topics for materials and allows them to show their creativity and ingenuity. Students could also work in groups or individually in creating materials. As they observe other students using materials they have used, students feel a sense of satisfaction and a boost in self-esteem.

Community-derived resources. One rich and extensive source of materials is the community, which offers many types of free or inexpensive materials. Any business or government office/ agency (local, state, or federal) is a potential source for classroom materials. Forms, booklets, pamphlets, applications (job, housing, utility service, medical/ dental histories, services, Social Security, food stamps, voter registration), checks and deposit/ withdrawal slips from a bank, restaurant menus, apartment/housing guides, postal forms, phone books, maps from realty offices, menus from restaurants (fast food, sit-down, cafeterias, snack bars),

drivers' manuals from the department of motor vehicles, mall maps and directories, and newspapers are a gold mine of educational materials that are available at little or no cost.

Materials can also be solicited from students, parents, family members, teachers, and the school's parent organization. Materials such as magazines, empty boxes and containers, "junk mail," catalogs, or coupons can be used to make file folder or teaching packets. Anything that has the potential of teaching or demonstrating a skill used in everyday living is valuable to a life skills teacher. The list of items that can be collected from community sources or individuals can be lengthy, but it ensures that the materials used are community specific.

Real-Life Technology

Technology has become a significant part of our daily lives. The impact is felt in all parts of our lives, jobs, home, community, and education. Teachers who address life skills topics need to incorporate into their lessons whenever possible the technology found in everyday environments. Automatic teller machines (ATM), answer machines, microwaves, automated gas pumps with debit/credit options, cordless/cellular phones, VCR, compact discs, personal computers and notebooks, computerized dictionaries and thesauruses, facsimile machines, and remote controls for the garage, TV, and VCR are samples of technology we encounter daily.

GUIDELINES FOR SELECTING LIFE SKILLS MATERIALS

According to Hammill and Bartel (1990) much time has been devoted to determining the content of curriculum used in schools, deciding the evaluative techniques used to determine individual needs of students, and selecting the teaching methods used. They estimate that, by comparison, little time is spent selecting instructional materials. In addition, Hammill and Bartel suggest that between 75% and 99% of the instructional student's time is arranged around some type of material. They propose that materials need to be chosen carefully to ensure that they are compatible with the curriculum, the student, and the teacher.

Selecting/evaluating materials. Hammill and Bartel (1990) caution teachers to select materials wisely, as many are designed to meet the needs of groups of students, not one specific student. Accommodating students' needs becomes imperative when their functioning level deviates from the targeted audience for the material. It becomes even more important to develop criterion for selection of materials when using a life skills curriculum to ensure the material will address the adult outcome objectives, interest level, reading level, etc. reflected in the student's IEP/ITP.

Many professionals have suggested ways of selecting and evaluating educational material (Clark & Kolstoe, 1990; Gast, 1987; Hammill & Bartel, 1990; Mastropieri & Scruggs, 1987; Mercer & Mercer, 1989; Woodward & Peters, 1983). Some checklists and forms ask as little as five or six questions to evaluate the material while others consist of two to three pages of numerous questions to consider. Several evaluation forms suggest specific variables (cost, readability, target age, durability, task

levels, interest levels, format, sequence and organization of the material, clarity of directions) (Gast, 1987; Mastropieri & Scruggs, 1987; Mercer & Mercer, 1989; Woodward & Peters, 1983). Others include an overall evaluative approach that considers the adaptability of the material for the student(s), laterality of instruction (Gast, 1987), compatibility of the material with the learning theory of the teacher and learning style of the student(s) (Clark & Kolstoe, 1990). We suggest using a combination of the above to evaluate a material used to teach a life skill.

A thorough examination of the variables in analyzing the materials has been suggested in Hammill and Bartel (1990). Figure 4.2 from Hammill and Bartel lists items to consider when the teacher is purchasing a material. Several of the 10 factors suggested should be addressed when any material, whether purchased, teacher-made, or community-based, is being considered for use with specific students. Knowing such information as the level of the material, format, and time requirements will impact the success of using that material with students.

In addition to the 10 items suggested by Hammill and Bartel, we would like to suggest an 11th one. Review the material for bias, stereotyping, and discrimination. Having the material reflect diversity as to gender, race, and disability is important. Students need to see the material as relevant to them, to their environment, and to their envisioning themselves performing life skills in their community. Materials also need to reflect our society's diversity.

Figure 4.3 lists the variables relating to the curriculum-student-teacher triad (Hammill & Bartel, 1990), which is referred to earlier in this chapter. These variables are important to consider when trying to match the material to the content being taught as well as the academic and cultural needs and functioning level of the student. Teachers also need to consider the method used and the time involved in using the material. In addition, some materials involve training and education on the part of the teacher that are not always feasible. Utilizing both the materials analysis and evaluation of the curriculum-student-teacher triad would be a good start in customizing an appropriate review in selecting life skill materials.

Materials Analysis

1. **Bibliographic and price information.** This information is necessary for future reference or purchase, as well as to make determinations that may assist in analysis. The teacher may consider such items as:

   Title—The name of the product may help identify the content area and whether the product is part of a set or series.

   Author—Is it someone known for his or her work in a specific area or someone associated with a particular approach?

   Copyright—Is it current? Will the work reflect new trends and facts?

   Price—Is it within the budget limitations? Is it in keeping with other materials prices and does it appear reasonable for the work's teaching value?

   Publisher—Does the company have a reputation for producing a certain kind or quality of material? Does the company support its products through staff development and services for purchasers?

2. **Instructional area and skills, scope and sequence.** Does the material cover the content area or specific components of the area? Does it address the specific skills needed? Does the material present initial instruction, remediation, and practice and/or reinforcement activities for the skills? Are the skills presented in the appropriate sequence? Is each skill given an equal amount of coverage?

3. **Component parts of the material.** Are there multiple pieces to the material? Can the pieces be used independently? Can the pieces be used for other purposes? Are there consumable pieces? Can the pieces be purchased independently? Will it be a problem to keep track of all components?

Figure 4.2. Materials Analysis. From *Teaching Students with Learning and Behavior Problems* (pp. 541–542) by Donald D. Hammill and Nettie R. Bartel, 1990. Boston: Allyn and Bacon. Copyright 1990 by Allyn and Bacon. Reprinted with permission.

4. **Level of the material.** Does the publisher state the readability level of the material? Is it consistent throughout the material? Is there more than one book for each level? Is there an attempt tocontrol the use of content-specific vocabulary? Is the interest level appropriate to the content, pictures, and publisher's statements?

5. **Quality.** Is the material (e.g., paper, tape, acetate, film, etc.) of good and durable quality? Is the print clear and of appropriate size and contrast with the background color? Are the illustrations clear and relevant to content? Do they add to rather than detract from the instruction?

6. **Format.** Is the form appropriate (e.g., workbook, slide, tape, etc.)? Does it utilize the appropriate receptive and expressive modes for the content? Is the material clear and easy to follow? Is special equipment required (e.g., projector, recorder, etc.)?

7. **Support materials.** Are there additional components besides the instructional items used by the child (e.g., placement tests, check-tests, resource files, objective clusters)? Are there teacher's guides and/or teacher's editions? Are there teacher-training materials?

8. **Time requirements.** Are the tasks of an appropriate length? Does the material allow flexibility for scheduling? Does it allow flexibility in instructional procedures?

9. **Field test and research data.** Does the publisher offer any research that would support the validity or reliability of the material? Are there any data to support either process or product studies? In essence, do the data support the contention that the material will do what the publisher says it will do for the type of student indicated?

10. **Method, approach, or theoretical bases.** Does the material utilize a specific approach or method, or is it based on a specific theoretical concept? Is it one that meets the needs of the triad? Is it compatible with other ongoing instruction? Is the method, approach, or basic theory substantiated by any published research?

Figure 4.2. *Continued*

Student Variables

1. **Needs of the student.** What skills and concepts are required of the student for immediate success?

2. **Current level of functioning.** What is the student's level of performance within the sequence of skills? What is the student's current reading level for instructional purposes?

3. **Grouping.** How well does the student work in groups of varying size (e.g., in small groups, in large groups, individually)?

4. **Programming.** What is the best arrangement for presentation to the student? Can the student work independently? Is the student self-directed and motivated? Does the student require direct teaching and/or frequent reinforcement?

5. **Methods.** Is there a history of success or failure with any particular methods? Does the student react positively or negatively to particular modes of instruction (e.g., multimedia versus print only)?

6. **Physical, social, and psychological characteristics.** Are there characteristics that imply unique needs (e.g., orthopedic restrictions, family problems, ethnic or cultural diversity, etc.)?

Teacher Variables

1. **Method.** What method does the teacher want to employ? What is the teacher's philosophy toward the teaching of particular content?

2. **Approach.** What approach is required by the teacher and the teacher's organization (e.g., group instruction or individual instruction, a phonetic approach, etc.)?

3. **Time.** Does the teacher have specific and required time constraints for delivery of instruction? Does the teacher have someone else who can deliver the instruction?

4. **Training.** Has the teacher been trained to use certain materials?

5. **Education.** Has the teacher been trained to be competent in the content area, or will the teacher require that the material be all-inclusive?

Figure 4.3. Variables Related to the Curriculum-Student-Teacher Triad. From *Teaching Students with Learning and Behavior Problems* (pp. 537–539) by Donald D. Hammill and Nettie R. Bartel, 1990. Boston: Allyn and Bacon. Copyright 1990 by Allyn and Bacon. Reprinted with permission.

Identifying materials. One of the most difficult tasks for teachers is locating materials. We have tried to assist teachers in identifying different types of materials as indicated by Appendix A in this book. There are many other ways in addition to this type of listing that teachers use to locate instructional materials. Hammill and Bartel (1990) offer a list of other possible sources to serve as a guide for teachers in this pursuit. The following eight suggestions describe those options:

1. *Ask other colleagues.* Networking with other life skills teachers will help you identify what they use with students who are working on skills similar to your students'.

2. *Seek help from special resource personnel.* These individuals devote most of their time to reviewing materials and media for classroom use and have access to individuals who are using similar materials. They also know several representatives of publishing companies. They may be librarians, media/materials specialists, or curriculum coordinators.

3. *Locate information from publishers.* Access catalogs, mailed brochures, and/or representatives of publishing companies. Many companies have toll-free numbers that you can call to have a catalog sent to you. Most companies publish new catalogs at the beginning of the school year or in January. Note that price and availability are always subject to change.

4. *Visit the nearest media/materials centers.* Identify the local or regional media center servicing your school. The centers house various collections of materials and will let teachers "borrow" the materials to use in their classrooms in an attempt to evaluate that material with their class prior to purchasing it. This is a cost-effective and efficient way of evaluating materials.

5. *Avail yourself to the resources of a college/university.* Many colleges and universities have a resource center or courses in methods and materials. Some faculty members may be involved in the field testing of particular materials.

6. *Locate prepared material lists.* Lists can be found in teacher resource books or textbooks, disseminated during workshops or conference sessions, or requested from school districts or state departments of education. Most of these lists include basic information only. They normally do not evaluate materials.

7. *Attend conferences.* Sessions and exhibits at conferences can provide an opportunity to look at the material itself. They also provide the chance for teachers to confer with each other regarding materials used in their classes.

8. *Use a computerized retrieval system.* Retrieval systems are generally developed by commercial companies and provide information on the physical characteristics of the materials, cost, availability, etc. This chapter outlines some considerations teachers need to address when identifying, selecting, and developing materials for use in their life skills programs. Attention to this process of acquiring materials will, hopefully, assure the best possible tools for teaching students life skills concepts. (p. 539–540)

Programming for Adult Outcomes: Life Skills Assessment and Transition Planning

To plan programs for secondary students with special needs, teachers need to determine the students' level of functioning in all programming areas. Those areas include academics, vocational aptitude and interest, social skills, study skills, and life skill competence. Each of these areas is important to the students' success in several subsequent environments. The areas are also dependent on outcome-based programming and learning. In addition, appropriate assessment is essential in planning transition programs in all areas but especially in determining a student's knowledge level of application of basic life skills.

Many variables contribute to the success of any student's program. This chapter addresses the components of program development that can make the difference in successfully implementing a life skills curriculum, that is, the assessment of life skills and planning for transition.

ASSESSING STUDENT LIFE SKILLS COMPETENCE

Assessing the life skill competencies of students is an important component in planning programs at the secondary level. Determining the level of any skill is imperative in order to identify the instructional level of the student. In addition, the assessment of life skills should be part of the total assessment picture at the secondary level that should take place at least 2 to 3 years prior to exiting school. Life skill assessment should continue throughout those exit years, as life skill preparation for transition to life after high school is an ongoing process. This section will discuss the measurement of life skills and the available assessment procedures to do so.

Commercially Available Assessment Measures

There are few commercially available assessment measures. Table 5.1, Commercially Available Life Skill Assessment Measures, gives a synopsis of selected commercially available instruments. We suggest that anyone considering any of the instruments listed do a review of their students' needs, the content of the curriculum in use, and the purpose of the instrument to determine the appropriateness of using the instrument. The instruments reviewed in the table include the *Life Centered Career Education Competency Rating Scale* (Brolin, 1991), the *Normative Adaptive Behavior Checklist* (Adams, 1986), the *Tests of Everyday Living* (Halpern, Irvin, & Landman, 1979), the *National Independent Living Skills Screening Instrument* (Sands, Woosley, & Dunlap, 1985), the *Street Survival Skills Questionnaire* (Linkenhoker & McCarron, 1980), and the *Test of Practical Knowledge* (Wiederholt & Larsen, 1983).

We want to recognize the place and importance of normed referenced instruments. The information gained from the administration of normed referenced tests of life skills helps determine placement decisions and is used to plan long-term and transitional programs for students with special needs. The impact of formal testing on day-to-day planning and teaching is felt only by the placement decision made based on the results of the test data. Assessment for day-to-day planning, such as evaluating student progress and building more effective programs for individual students, involves an alternative to commerically distributed achievement tests (Deno, 1985; Wood, 1992). The next section describes and gives examples of how the curriculum-based assessment concept can be utilized in a life skills program.

TABLE 5.1. Commercially Available Life Skill Assessment Measures

Test	Purpose	Features	Subtests	Target Audience
Normative Adaptive Behavior Checklist	Identifies individuals with adaptive behavior deficits, provides a norm-referenced evaluation of skills and abilities, and identifies individuals needing more evaluation.	• Standard scores • Age equivalents • Percentiles	• Self Help • Home Living • Independent Living • Social Skills • Sensory Motor • Language Concepts	1–21.11 years
Street Survival Skills Questionnaire	Measures specific aspects of adaptive behavior of special education students used as a baseline behavioral measure of effects of training and to predict an individual's potential for successfully adapting to community living conditions and vocational placement.	• Standard scores • Individually administered	• Basic Concepts • Functional Signs • Tools • Domestics • Health & Safety • Public Service • Time • Monetary • Measurements	9–15.11 years
Tests for Everyday Living	Measures low-functioning students' knowledge of skills necessary for performing everyday activities.	• Compares mean and standard deviation with reference groups	• Purchasing Habits • Banking • Budgeting • Health Care • Home Management • Job Search Skills • Job Related Behavior	Grades 7–12
Test of Practical Knowledge	Identifies high school students who are less knowledgeable than their peers about important daily living skills. Determines strengths and weaknesses and documents student progress.	• Standard scores • Percentile ranks • Practical Knowledge Quotient	• Social • Personal • Occupational	12.11–18.8 years Grades 8–12
Life Centered Career Education Competency Rating Scale	CBA used to measure the career education knowledge and skills of special education students. Used to determine instructional goals.	• Not standardized but has had extensive field testing	• Daily Living • Personal/Social • Occupational	Grades 7–12
National Independent Living Skills Screening Instrument	Estimates an individual's knowledge base and current independent living skills level in each of the 7 skill areas.	• Uses both interview and direct observation formats	• Health/Hygiene • Family Responsibility • Money Management • Community Awareness • Legal Awareness • Social/Interpersonal Skills • Maladaptive Behavior	16+ years

Curriculum-Based Measures

Measures of students' performance in the context of the curriculum requirements of their classroom settings has been documented as the most useful way to assess student needs and progress (Durkin, 1984; Samuels, 1984). Curriculum-based assessment (CBA) has emerged to fill this need for an assessment process based on a student's progress through an individual curriculum (Wood, 1992).

The nature of life skills instruction (i.e., occurring in the community and utilizing instructional materials) lends itself more effectively to this type of assessment technique. A number of informal techniques used in CBA can be implemented to determine students' ability to perform a host of life skills competencies. The steps to develop a CBA are listed in Figure 5.1. These steps suggested by Blankenship (1985) and Blankenship and Lily (1981) and adapted by Wood (1992) are simple to follow. When using CBA for the first time, start slowly developing a CBA with one life skill at a time. This can be done as individual students are working on specific life skills. As you develop life skill CBAs, exchange CBAs with other teachers of life skills to help build your life skill CBA files in many areas for future use.

Table 5.2, Curriculum-Based Measurement Procedures by Adult Domains, outlines the various methods of informal assessment that can be used with selected life skills in each of the adult domains. The selected life skills used in Table 5.2 were chosen from the sample life skills outlined in Figures 3.4 and 3.5, the Elementary and Secondary Matrices respectively, and from the top-down process depicted in Figure 2.3. The sample goal, related test item pool, and measurement procedure are built on the life skill representing each adult domain. The goals, item pool, and measurement procedures are meant to illustrate the typical ones used in a CBA for measurement of life skill competence.

Steps for Using Curriculum-Based Assessment

1. List the skills presented in the selected material.

2. Make sure all important skills are presented.

3. Decide if the skills are in logical order.

4. Write an objective for each skill on the list.

5. Prepare items to test each objective.

6. Prepare the test.

7. Plan how the CBA will be given.

8. Give the CBA immediately before instruction on a topic.

9. Study the results to determine:
   a. Which students have already mastered the skills?
   b. Which students have the prerequisite skills to begin instruction?
   c. Which students don't have prerequisite skills?

10. Readminister the CBA after instruction to determine:
    a. Which students have mastered the skills and are ready to move to a new topic?
    b. Which students need more practice?
    c. Which students need additional instruction?
    d. Which students need modifications in the curriculum?

11. Readminister the CBA throughout the year to test for long-term mastery.

Figure 5.1. Steps for Using Curriculum-Based Assessment (CBA). From ''Using Curriculum-based Assessment Data to Make Instructional Decisions'' by C. S. Blankenship, 1985, *Exceptional Children, 52,* p. 234. Copyright 1985 by The Council for Exceptional Children. Adapted by permission. Original Source: Blankenship, C. S. (1985). ''Assessment, Curriculum, and Instruction.'' In J. F. Cawley (Ed.), *Practical Mathematics Appraisal of the Learning Disabled* (pp. 59–79), Austin, TX: PRO-ED; Blankenship, C., & Lilly, M. S. (1981). *Mainstreaming Students with Learning and Behavior Problems: Techniques for the Classroom Teacher,* New York: Holt, Rinehart & Winston.

TABLE 5.2. Curriculum-Based Measurement Procedures by Adult Domains

	Simple Goal	*Related Test Item Materials*	*Measurement Procedure*
Employment/ Education	Given a local newspaper's classified ads, the student will locate 3 entry-level jobs appropriate for their skills level and interest with 100% accuracy.	local newspaper classified ads	Provide the classified section of the local newspaper. Direct the student to locate 3 job openings appropriate to their skills and interest; score performance if student locates 3 job openings of appropriate skill and interest level.
Home and Family	Given $10 and 7 items selected at a grocery store for purchase, the student will total the cost of all items and determine if $10 will cover the cost with 100% accuracy.	7 grocery store items	Randomly select items from grocery store shelves. Present the student with items and a small hand calculator; provide directions; score performance if student correctly determines that $10 will cover the cost of all 7 items.
Leisure Pursuits	Given a local weather broadcast on radio or TV, the student will determine if an outdoor activity is appropriate with 100% accuracy.	radio or TV	Provide the student a radio or TV to listen for a weather broadcast; direct student to listen for the weather forecast to see if they should plan an outdoor activity; score performance if student makes an appropriate decision based on outdoor activity and current weather conditions.
Community Involvement	Given a pencil and blank local voter registration card, the student will complete the form with 100% accuracy.	local voter registration form	Provide the student with a blank voter registration form; direct student to fill out form completely; score performance if student fills in all blanks correctly.
Physical/Emotional Health	Given a local phone book and the direction to find the phone number of the poison control center, the student will locate and write down the number and tape it to the phone with 100% accuracy.	phone book, tape, pencil, paper, telephone	Provide the student with a local phone book with the directions to find the number of the poison control center; write it down and tape on phone; score performance if student finds either the local poison control number and/or the national 800 number, correctly writes the number on paper and tapes to phone.
Personal Responsibility and Relationships	Given stationery, envelope, pen, and a stamp, the student will write an appropriate thank-you note, including address, for a gift with 100% accuracy.	stationery, envelope, pen, stamp	Provide student with stationery, envelope, pen, and stamp; direct student to write an appropriate thank-you note, including addressing envelope, for a gift they have received; score performance if student writes an appropriate note, including all essential elements such as date, salutation, mention of gift, appreciation for gift, closing, their name, and envelope addressed correctly.

INDIVIDUAL PROGRAM PLANNING

The relationship between assessment and planning should be very close. Measures of life skills functioning that produce useful information should lead to accurate statements of current levels of performance. Knowing what a student can do allows teachers to develop appropriate goals and objectives that can be written into the student's educational program.

Individualized Education Program (IEP)

The individualized education program (IEP) serves as the "management tool that is used to ensure that each student is provided special education and related services appropriate to address identified learning needs" (Strickland & Turnbull, 1990, p. 13). By law, every IEP must contain the following components:

- current levels of performance
- annual goals
- short-term objectives
- special education services to be provided
- related services to be provided
- extent of time student will be in regular education settings
- dates for initiation and duration of services
- criteria for evaluating short-term objectives

From examining Figures 3.4 and 3.5, the matrices showing the relationship between scholastic/social skills and life skills, it is obvious that many life skills can be included as academic or behavioral goals/objectives of students' IEPs. For instance, an annual goal in math focusing on measurement can easily be related to a life skill need.

The inclusion of life skills goals and objectives in IEPs helps assure that students are taught these important topics. Unfortunately, studies that examined the content of IEPs have consistently found that very few goals and corresponding objectives related to career development and life skills are listed in students' IEPs.

The Individuals with Disabilities Education Act (IDEA) of 1990 (P.L. 101-476) now requires that the IEP include a statement of needed transition services. A statement of transition services and the identification of various interagency responsibilities must be part of the IEP of all students before they are 16 years old. The law defines transition services [20 U.S.C. 1401(a) (19)] as

> a coordinated set of activities for a student, designed within an outcome-oriented process, which promotes movement from school to postschool activities including postsecondary education, vocational training, integrated employment (including supported employment), continuing and adult education, adult services, independent living or community participation.

Although this requirement is extremely important, it is very possible that many important areas of adult functioning may still be overlooked. For this reason, comprehensive transition plans are likely to be more valuable to students. Whether such documents exist is a function of the school system in which students find themselves.

Individual Transition Plans (ITP)

A comprehensive individual transition plan (ITP) should address the major areas for which students need to be prepared prior to leaving school. Frequently, this might involve establishing linkages with postschool services; other times, it might suggest teaching students specific skills that they will need in their subsequent environments. Sample ITPs that have been developed and are being used in various parts of the United States are provided in Appendix G.

The ITP format that we propose is based on the six domains of adulthood depicted in Figure 2.2. Although the content is different, the format of the ITP is a derivation of the ITP developed by the Hawaii Transition Project and is similar to the ITP used by the Hawaii Department of Education. The actual planning component of our proposed ITP is depicted in Figure 5.2; additional components such as student information and the signatures of people participating in the development of the ITP are not shown. As Figure 5.2 shows, the four distinguishing features of the ITP are

- the transition service area (i.e., adult domain);

- the person/agency responsible for accomplishing the goal;

- an indication when the activities associated with a particular goal will be started; and

- a comments column that can be used in a number of ways, such as indicating the status of a particular goal (e.g., "completed").

TRANSITION SERVICE AREAS	PERSON/AGENCY RESPONSIBLE	TIMELINE	COMMENTS
A. Employment/Education Goal:			
B. Home and Family Goal:			
C. Leisure Pursuits Goal:			

PERSON(S) RESPONSIBLE: **F**-Family   **S**-School   **A**-Agency   **ST**-Students
COMMENTS: **I**-Initiated   **C**-Completed   **R**-Revised   **O**-Others

Figure 5.2. Individual Transition Plan. *(continues on p. 54)*

TRANSITION SERVICE AREAS	PERSON/AGENCY RESPONSIBLE	TIMELINE	COMMENTS
D. Community Involvement Goal:			
E. Emotional/Physical Health Goal:			
F. Personal Responsibility and Relationships Goal:			
PERSON(S) RESPONSIBLE: F-Family S-School A-Agency ST-Students **COMMENTS:** I-Initiated C-Completed R-Revised O-Others			

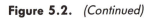

Figure 5.2. *(Continued)*

Developing Life Skills Goals and Objectives

As emphasized earlier in this chapter, the actual goals and objectives to be included in a student's ITP will be determined after assessing needs. Once needs have been established, goals need to be developed. One possible way to do this is to consult the list of major life demands presented in Table 2.2. We feel that these demands can usually serve as goal statements, and the short-term objectives can be generated from a careful analysis of the specific life skills associated with each major life demand.

Two examples of this process for developing goals and objectives are provided. To demonstrate this process, a brief description of each student's situation is presented (i.e., partial assessment report) and then a sample ITP is offered. *(Please see pp. 56–57.)*

Scenario #1:
17-year-old female; highly motivated; significant problems in written expression; interested in pursuing a career in nursing. Probable subsequent environment: attend school away from home; live on campus; will not have a car.

Jennifer Kelly			p. 1 of 2
TRANSITION SERVICE AREAS	PERSON/AGENCY RESPONSIBLE	TIMELINE	COMMENTS
A. Employment/Education Goal: Gain entry to postsecondary education setting.	Student, parents, Transition Coordinator	By admission deadline	Information and selection criteria needed.
B. Home and Family Goal: Establish good credit	parents	June — after graduation	Consider applying for credit card
C. Leisure Pursuits Goal: Perform individual physical activities	Physical education teacher	November of school year	Discuss community resources, their locations, and costs
PERSON(S) RESPONSIBLE: F-Family S-School A-Agency ST-Students COMMENTS: I-Initiated C-Completed R-Revised O-Others			

Jennifer Kelly			p. 2 of 2
TRANSITION SERVICE AREAS	PERSON/AGENCY RESPONSIBLE	TIMELINE	COMMENTS
D. Community Involvement Goal: Access public transportation	Student, Parents, Teacher	February of school year	Contact transportation services in cities where apply for college
E. Emotional/Physical Health Goal: Manage stress	Teacher, Counselor	September of school year	Identify support services in college settings
F. Personal Responsibility and Relationships Goal: Establish and maintain friendships	Teacher, student	March of school year	Explore social organizations and extracurricular offerings at selected college
PERSON(S) RESPONSIBLE: F-Family S-School A-Agency ST-Students COMMENTS: I-Initiated C-Completed R-Revised O-Others			

Figure 5.3. Individual Transition Plan.

Scenario #2:

16-year-old male; tired of school—wants to get a job; reading skills are adequate; math skills are weak; also has some problems relating appropriately to peers; interested in finding a job working in a warehouse. Probable subsequent environment: work in nearby community; live at home; will have a car.

DAVID RYAN			P. 1
TRANSITION SERVICE AREAS	**PERSON/AGENCY RESPONSIBLE**	**TIMELINE**	**COMMENTS**
A. Employment/Education Goal: Seek and secure a job	Transition Coordinator, Student	January of school year	Prepare career planning packet. Identify job sites.
B. Home and Family Goal: Prepare for marriage and family	Teacher	October of school year	Identify community resources
C. Leisure Pursuits Goal: Attend special neighborhood events	Teacher, Student	September of school year	Link interests with local options.
PERSON(S) RESPONSIBLE: F-Family S-School A-Agency ST-Students **COMMENTS:** I-Initiated C-Completed R-Revised O-Others			

DAVID RYAN			P. 2
TRANSITION SERVICE AREAS	**PERSON/AGENCY RESPONSIBLE**	**TIMELINE**	**COMMENTS**
D. Community Involvement Goal: Know about wide range of services available in the community	Teacher	December of school year	Use community-based experiences.
E. Emotional/Physical Health Goal: Seek personal counseling	Counselor, Teacher	October of school year	Locate and contact community services.
F. Personal Responsibility and Relationships Goal: Get along with others.	Teacher, Transition Coordinator	January of school year	Identify interpersonal job skills required in warehouse setting.
PERSON(S) RESPONSIBLE: F-Family S-School A-Agency ST-Students **COMMENTS:** I-Initiated C-Completed R-Revised O-Others			

Figure 5.4. Individual Transition Plan.

Specific Suggestions for Planning, Implementing, and Maintaining a Life Skills Program

Curricular change can be exciting and challenging for everyone—administrators, parents, and teachers. Small-scale change can take place with one student or class, or change can be system-wide involving all schools. The options for teaching life skills, as noted in Figure 3.1, provide a sense of the various levels on which life skills can be integrated into a students' programs. Regardless of how extensively life skills are taught in school, the variables discussed in this chapter will be relevant and valuable in setting up any program.

In reviewing programs that have undergone curricular change, several points surface that need to be examined by those considering modification or alteration to their present program. One frequent suggestion is to allocate time for adequate program preparation, which will allow for a smooth transition into the new curriculum/program. Part of that preparation is identifying the stages that can be investigated prior to attempting any program change. Those stages include several steps to follow before getting started, while implementing the program, and during program maintenance. Devoting time and attention to these variables will significantly contribute to the potential success of a program. A short discussion of important variables to deliberate during each one of these phases follows.

GETTING STARTED

In the initial stages of considering a curriculum change, many steps should be deliberated by the decision makers. Several of these steps will save time and energy in the long run. Many of them will also strengthen the program.

Administrative support (district and school-based). One of the most important and integral support variables you can have is the administration at all levels—school-based, district, and state. Many times if administrators support the premise of the program, they can be instrumental in accessing monies—regular budget, grant, and private donations. They will also be your advocates in the community and with parents. Having them understand the nature of the program will also help when it comes time to go on a field experience. In addition, having your principal support your program at the district or even the state levels can lead to participation on panels, conference presentations, and involvement in systems change at the district or state level.

Additional funding. Additional funding will always enhance the program. Monies can be used to pay teachers for their time in developing the program, extra in-service days; setting up new classrooms, building a life skills material library, and the additional expenses associated with field experiences. All states offer grants for which school systems or individual schools can apply. These are usually for 1, 2, or 3 years of funding. Cooperative grants can also be submitted with other agencies, such as a university, to train personnel how to develop life skills programs in their classes, schools, or districts. In addition, cooperative grants can also be submitted to develop demonstration sites.

Teacher willingness to try something new. Teachers who are successful in developing and teaching a life skills program are many times willing to try something new, different, and challenging. These individuals see the connection between what they are doing in the classroom and their students' probable subsequent environments. They realize that potentially a major programming change to focusing on adult outcomes will make a difference in their students' lives.

Teacher involvement in the development of the curriculum. Teacher involvement is invaluable in a program like this. When teachers take ownership of a program, success is not far behind. The investment they make, both professionally and personally, is evident in their students' excitement about learning adult skills.

Student input. We have found that one of the most motivating factors for students is their active involvement in the program. Involvement includes creating materials, finding field experience sites, making decisions on what they learn next, and attending their own IEP/ITP meeting. Whatever the level of involvement, excitement and motivation for learning life skills will be evident.

Start small—pilot class. Programs have to begin somewhere. We have found that it is best to start small. A pilot class or one school is best. Many things can be learned from the mistakes made in one situation before going school-wide or system-wide.

Lifelong learning. Another aspect that we strive to teach students in a life skills program is the awareness that learning never ends. Learning doesn't stop at 3 p.m. or on Friday or in May or June or when they receive their diploma. Learning continues every moment of every day.

Improving quality of life. One of the most important benefits of a life skills program is the constant improvement of the students' quality of life, which has a permanent, positive effect on their life.

Scheduling preparation time. Teachers need time during the day to contact resource people, find field experiences, or search for materials. In addition, time is needed to prepare lessons, complete paperwork, coordinate materials, and meet with the students.

Providing faculty with opportunity to customize curriculum. Time is needed to develop life skills programs. Collaboration with other teachers interested in life skills will enrich the program and ensure that it is locally and culturally referenced. Alternative times usually include after-school hours, weekends, and summers. Many school systems will give teachers compensation (time or money) for time spent developing programs on weekends and during the summer.

IMPLEMENTING

While many variables should be considered when making programmatic changes, several factors are especially important during the initial stages of implementing a curriculum. The success of this phase will make a difference in continuing past the program's initial academic year.

Make content adult/community referenced. Content of the life skills program should reflect the tasks expected of the adults in the community in which the students live. These factors will increase student interest and motivation in learning. In addition, the life skill tasks should reflect the culture familiar to the students and the cultures represented in their community.

Include community-based experiences in instruction. Exploring the community through field experiences will also increase interest and motivation and give relevancy to the academic tasks performed in school. In addition, students will experience the powerful impact of learning by doing.

Utilize the local community. Students should be familiar with the community in which they will live the greater part, if not all, of their lives. When members of the community visit the school, students have the opportunity to learn about different jobs, services, and cultures in addition to meeting the individuals who may be the students' future employers.

Content must be relevant. As stated several times in this text, content must be relevant to the students and their cultures. If content is relevant to the students, they are less likely to drop out. In addition, they see the value of learning for a lifetime.

Relate content to students' probable subsequent experiences and environments. In setting up an outcome-based program, one must be cognizant of the probable subsequent environments in which the students will be functioning. There should be a match between the tasks expected in the subsequent environments and the tasks being taught in school. This should be the driving force of any life skill program.

Provide testimonials. Former students can emphasize the importance of learning life skills in school with support from the teachers. They can attest to the fact that it is easier than the trial-and-error method. There is nothing more valuable than former students telling students to stay in school. This can be a powerful motivator for not dropping out.

Set up a series of workshops. Staff training can be an essential element in effective implementation of a program. It is crucial for teachers to be trained in teaching life skills. Many programs deteriorate or even fail because time is neither taken to train new staff each year nor to provide ongoing assistance for veteran teachers.

Encourage teachers to form a support group. Support groups can be the element that keeps the life skills program together. The purpose of a support group should be to meet the needs of its members. In a life skills program, this could mean networking ideas, sharing names of resource people, exchanging information on potential field experience sites, identifying sources of materials (available both commercially and in the community), venting frustrations, and seeking solutions to problems that will occur in any program.

Develop a school, district-wide, or state-wide newsletter. This method of communication may be in addition to or instead of a support group. In some situations it may not be feasible to form a support group that meets on a regular basis. Distance and time could make it difficult for groups to meet frequently or even at all. A newsletter is a way of meeting life skills teachers' need to communicate with each other. Again, it is another way to keep informed and share ideas, contacts, and sources.

Earn money. Many, if not most, programs need a certain amount of petty cash to keep the field experience component of the life skills program active. Money for public transportation, purchasing food and drink from vending machines, fast food places, or the occasional lunch out for the class is sometimes needed. School money-making projects such as bake sales, candy sales, selling personalized computer-generated greeting cards during holiday seasons, or car washes can provide the needed cash for these important excursions.

Continue involvement of students. It is essential for students to continue being involved in the program. Their contribution to and ownership of the program is invaluable. Teachers should encourage their continued involvement in decisions, suggestions for field experiences, gathering materials from the community or home, and choices of which life skill to attempt next.

Involve parents. Involved parents on any level are important to the success of a program. The type of involvement may be limited due to job or family, but it can still happen. Ask parents to collect life skills materials, suggest field experiences or use their places of employment, invite them to the class as resource people, share other hobbies or leisure time interests, accompany the class on a field experience, or help with a workshop or the newsletter.

KEEPING THE PROGRAM GOING

After a program is up and running for a few years, several variables will keep the program going and strengthen it over time. It is easy to become complacent and just maintain status quo. But a life skills program continues to change as the students and community change. Keep the following recommendations in mind after your program has been operating several years.

Continue revising. This will be a continual process as a teacher works with a program or curriculum. Including new concepts and taking out old ones will ensure an up-to-date program.

Follow up with graduates. Following up on the status of graduates will give feedback as to the aspects of the curriculum that influenced their success or problems they are having. This information will help you revise the curriculum to better meet the needs of the subsequent environments of future students.

Continue contact with the community. This will ensure that the program remains in close touch with the individuals who will be eventually working with students. This should be in addition to the teachers' continued use of the community for materials and field experiences that are locally and culturally referenced.

Apply for grants. Submission of applications for grant monies will give the program a better chance for the financial stability needed for longevity.

Seek monies from community or civic groups. Call upon community and civic groups such as those listed in Appendix C for help with short-term or petty cash projects. Many have funds that need to be disbursed annually. Several of these groups target schools or educational programs as benefactors of their organizations.

Continue focus on adult outcomes. Teachers should never lose sight of the purpose of a life skills curriculum—to focus on the acquisition of adult skills.

Teach as though each day is the last time you will see the students. For many students, this will be the last formal school experience they have. Some will be dropped from school by the system for various reasons. Others will self-exit or drop out. However it happens, as teachers of students with special needs or those who are at high risk, we know at the end of every day that the possibility exists that there may be a student or some students who will never return to school. We cannot forget the importance of our position as teachers of life skills. It is our job to teach every student, every day as if it were the last day they would be taught by us or any teacher.

This chapter offered teachers some guidelines and practical hints for starting, maintaining, and keeping a program going. We hope these suggestions provide a logical guide for those who develop life skills curricula.

Final Thoughts

The main theme of this guide is the importance of preparing youth with special needs for the challenges of adulthood. Our experiences suggest that many of the skills needed to enhance one's quality of life must be systematically addressed within the school curriculum. To do this effectively, a number of actions must occur. First, an examination of the subsequent environments to which students likely will go after they exit school should be conducted (Kortering & Elrod, 1991). Second, the curricular needs of students should be based upon this analysis (i.e., a top-down approach to curriculum development).

The principle purpose of the guide is to give teachers and other curriculum developers a methodology for integrating life skills topics into the educational programs of students. By providing a model and the resources that may be needed to implement it, we feel that locally referenced and culturally responsive life skills can be identified and, ultimately, taught.

THE VALUE OF LIFE SKILLS PREPARATION FOR ALL STUDENTS

All students—not just those with special needs—need to acquire requisite life skills. The major

demands of life, as discussed in Chapter 2, confront all of us. The difference is that many of us learn how to deal with them in a variety of ways—most notably through natural support systems. For many students with special needs, these support systems do not exist, so they may never learn some very important life skills.

It is unrealistic, even in the best life skills program imaginable, to prepare students for every possible adult situation. However, it is possible to attend to many of the more probable ones. Because we cannot precisely foresee students' future experiences, it is very important to build a strong problem-solving component into programs. Teaching students strategies that they can use to handle new, difficult situations provides them with tools they can use throughout their lives.

As stressed before, life skills preparation should begin at the elementary school level. Waiting until the last years of high school to get students ready for what lies ahead is ineffective and unconscionable. The Division on Career Development of the Council for Exceptional Children (Clark, Carlson, Fisher, Cook, & D'Alonzo, 1991) argues that

A commitment to life-centered career development and transition preparation for students exclusively at the secondary level is not only inadequate, it is counterproductive. Such an exclusive approach ignores the possibility that school programs have not succeeded in the past because of providing *too little, too late* [emphasis added]. (p. 118)

THE NEED FOR CURRICULAR INNOVATION

A number of professionals who are concerned about the plight of youth with special needs as they move into adulthood argue that curricular changes are needed to ensure better adult outcomes for these individuals. Three observations that ostensibly provide a strong rationale for promoting such changes follow.

> The truth is that the secondary curriculum for special education students appears to have very little, if any, impact on their eventual adjustment to community life. (Edgar, 1987, p. 560)

> The problem is that too many young people in public schools, particularly youths with disabilities and youths who are not college bound, are not well served by the traditional academic model. (Roessler, 1991, p. 59)

> Much of the curriculum that was being offered in the high schools could be characterized as an attempt to remediate basic academic skills and/or to provide intensive tutoring in the various content area subjects such as literature, social studies and science. Typically missing from the offerings were study skills or "learning strategies," and functional curricula aimed at independent living skills such as money management and meal preparation . . . . The impact of these curricular shortcomings was to deny a meaningful educational program for those who were not capable of succeeding in the regular academic curriculum. (Halpern, Benz, & Lindstrom, 1992, p. 111)

These comments describe the scenario for many students who are at risk for experiencing school failure and point out the need for re-evaluating the relationship between what students need to be taught and what is being taught.

Programs must be sensitive to students' current and future needs (Polloway, Patton, Epstein, & Smith, 1989). They need to be meaningful to students in the short-term to keep students in school, and they need to be relevant to students over the long term to help them function more successfully in their adult lives. As Wagner (1991) reports, the National Longitudinal Transition Study of Special Education (NLTS) findings imply "that if schools can give students powerful reasons to come to school and can help students achieve in their courses, they can help many students persist in school" (p. 108).

Throughout this guide, in our attempt to provide information to service providers to enable them to develop life skills programs, we have failed to emphasize the importance of involving students in their own life skills/transition planning. As Karge, Patton, and de la Garza (1992) conclude, "it is an inherent right to be involved in one's own life planning" (p. 65). Of course, such involvement is not always possible; however, for the vast majority of students with special needs, making decisions about their future is warranted.

Since dealing with the demands of adulthood is a lifelong venture, it is essential that we teach individuals with special needs to utilize ongoing support systems throughout their lives. This relates to the suggestion discussed earlier about teaching individuals to be functional problem solvers. The suggestion here is that some adults may need assistance in locating supports to help them to be successful. Edgar (1990) goes so far as to recommend that "we can replace teaching of skills with support of an individual" and that "by including ongoing support services as a possible intervention we do NOT give up instruction, rather we ADD an option to our intervention repertoire" (p. 13).

Because we live in a world that is changing very rapidly, those of us involved with life skills programming must address the realities of a complex world. Kolstoe's comments are as appropriate today as they were in 1976:

> Probably no final statement can ever be forthcoming concerning the skills and characteristics required to live successfully in this culture, primarily because society is characterized by constant change. . . . There seems, however, no alternative other than to use the best current information available for curricular guidelines and to modify those guidelines as new and better information becomes available. If society is constantly changing, it seems only reasonable that curricula should also change. (p. 33)

PERSONAL COMMITMENT TO STUDENTS

Most of us who teach or who have taught students at risk for school failure strive to provide skills and information to make their lives more enjoyable and fulfilling. Perhaps most importantly, we must strive to let these students know that we sincerely care about them and that they are important to us—which involves more than being an excellent teacher methodologically or a font of knowledge. It means that students should experience what Edgar (1990) calls "an atmosphere of caring, human dignity, and optimism" (p. 13).

Professionals concerned about what happens to students when formal schooling ends have to be alarmed by the outcome and dropout data that describes the fate of many individuals. We must keep advocating for students, always guided by their best interests. Edgar's (1991) notion that educators have a sacred covenant to students is most compelling:

> We must provide them with the best services, every day, that we can offer. We must think about how our efforts affect the student not only today but also in the future. We must step back, now and then, to look at the overall role of education, how we fit into the larger picture, and what changes we must make, in ourselves and in our system, so that our students will benefit from education. We must find ways to renew our own personal energy to keep doing this, day after day, year after year. It is our mission in life. (p. 39)

This guide for developing life skills instruction has evolved through this motivation.

References

Adams, G. L. (1986). *Normative Adaptive Behavior Check-list*. San Antonio, TX: Psychological Corporation.

Affleck, J., Edgar, E., Levine, P., & Kortering, L. (1990). Post-school status of students classified as mentally retarded. Does it get better with time? *Education and Training in Mental Retardation, 25,* 315–324.

Blankenship, C. S. (1985). Using curriculum-based assessment data to make instructional decisions. *Exceptional Children, 52,* 233–243.

Blankenship, C. S., & Lily, M. S. (1981). *Mainstreaming students with learning and behavior problems: Techniques for the classroom teacher.* New York: Holt, Reinhart, & Winston.

Blackorby, J., Edgar, E., & Kortering, L. J. (1991). A third of our youth? A look at the problems of high school dropout among students with mild handicaps. *Journal of Special Education, 25,* 102–113.

Brolin, D. (1978). *Life-centered career education: A competency-based approach.* Reston, VA: Council for Exceptional Children.

Brolin, D. (1991). *Life-centered career education: A competency-based approach* (3rd ed.). Reston, VA: Council for Exceptional Children.

Brolin, D. (1991). *Life-Centered Career Education Competency Rating Scale.* Reston, VA: Council for Exceptional Children.

Champlin, J. (1991). A powerful tool for school transformation. *The School Administrator, 48*(9), 34.

Clark, G. (1980). Career preparation for handicapped adolescents: A matter of appropriate education. *Exceptional Education Quarterly, 1*(2), 11–17.

Clark, G. M., Carlson, B. C., Fisher, S., Cook, I. D., & D'Alonzo, B. J. (1991). Career development for students with disabilities in elementary schools. A position statement on the Division on Career Development. *Career Development for Exceptional Individuals, 14,* 109–120.

Clark, G., & Kolstoe, O. (1990). *Career development and transition education for adolescents with disabilities.* Boston: Allyn & Bacon.

Cronin, M. E., Patton, J. R., & Polloway, E. A. (1991). *Preparing for adult outcomes: A model for developing a life skills curriculum.* Unpublished manuscript.

Deno, S. L. (1985). Curriculum-based assessment: The emergency alternative. *Exceptional Children, 52,* 219–232.

Dever, R. B. (1988). *Community living skills: A taxonomy.* Washington, DC: American Association on Mental Retardation.

Durkin, D. (1984). Is there a match between what elementary teachers do and what basal reader manuals recommend? *The Reading Teacher, 37,* 734–745.

Edgar, E. (1987). Secondary programs in special education: Are many of them justifiable? *Exceptional Children, 53*(6), 555–561.

Edgar, E. (1988). Employment as an outcome for mildly handicapped students: Current status and future direction. *Focus on Exceptional Children, 21*(1), 1–8.

Edgar, E. (1990). Education's role in improving the quality of life: Is it time to change our view of the world? *Beyond Behavior, 1*(1), 9–13.

Edgar, E. (1991). Providing ongoing support and making appropriate placements: An alternative to transition planning for mildly handicapped students. *Preventing School Failure, 35*(2), 36–39.

Friedland, S. (1992). Building student self-esteem for school improvement. *NASSP Bulletin, 76*(540), 96–102.

Gajar, A. (1992). Adults with learning disabilities: Current and future research priorities. *Journal of Learning Disabilities, 25,* 507–519.

Gast, K. B. (1987). Commercial curricula for the mildly handicapped: Consideration and review. *Teaching: Behaviorally Disordered Youth, 3,* 36–41.

Halpern, A. S., Benz, M. R., & Lindstrom, L. E. (1992). A systems change approach to improving secondary special education and transitions programs at the community level. *Career Development for Exceptional Individuals, 15,* 109–120.

Halpern, A., Irvin, L., & Landman, J. (1979). *Tests for Everyday Living.* Monterey, CA: CTB/McGraw-Hill.

Hammill, D. D., & Bartel, N. R. (1990). *Teaching students with learning and behavior problems.* Boston: Allyn and Bacon.

Hasazi, S. B., Gordon, L. B., & Roe, C. A. (1985). Factors associated with the employment status of handicapped youth exiting from high school from 1979 to 1983. *Exceptional Children, 51,* 455–469.

Hawaii Transition Project. (1987). Honolulu: Department of Special Education, University of Hawaii.

Karge, B. D., Patton, P. L., & de la Garza, B. (1992). Transition services for youth with mild disabilities: Do they exist, are they needed? *Career Development for Exceptional Individuals, 15,* 47–68.

King, J. A., & Evans, K. M. (1991). Can we achieve outcome-based education? *Educational Leadership, 49*(2), 73–75.

Kolstoe, O. P. (1976). *Teaching educable mentally retarded children* (2nd ed.). New York: Holt, Rinehart & Winston.

Kortering, L. J., & Elrod, G. F. (1991). Programs for mildly handicapped adolescents: Evaluating where we are contemplating change. *Career Development for Exceptional Individuals, 14,* 145–157.

Knowles, M. (1990). *The adult learner: The neglected species.* Houston: Gulf Publishing.

LaQuey, A. (1981). *Adult performance level adaptation and modification project.* Austin, TX: Educational Service Center, Region XIII.

Linkenhoker, D., & McCarron, L. (1980). *Street Survival Skills Questionnaire.* Dallas, TX: McCarron-Dial Systems.

Mastropieri, M. A., & Scruggs, T. E. (1987). *Effective instruction for special education.* Austin, TX: PRO-ED.

Mercer, C. D., & Mercer, A. R. (1989). *Teaching students with learning problems.* Columbus, OH: Merrill.

Mithaug, D. E., Horiuchi, C. N., & Fanning, P. N. (1985). A report on the Colorado statewide follow-up survey of special education students. *Exceptional Children, 51*(5), 397–404.

Moore, S. C., Agran, M., & McSweyn, C. A. (1990). Career education: Are we starting early enough? *Career Development for Exceptional Individuals, 13,* 129–134.

Murphy, S., & Walsh, J. (1989). Economics and the real-life connection. *Social Studies and the Young Learner, 2,* 6–8.

Neubert, D. A., & Foster, J. (1988). Learning disabled students make the transition. *Exceptional Children, 20*(3), 42–44.

Patton, J. R. (1986). *Transition: Curricular implications at the secondary level.* Honolulu: Project Ho'Okoho, Department of Special Education, University of Hawaii.

Patton, J. R., & Browder, P. (1988). Transitions into the future. In B. Ludlow, R. Luckasson, & A. Turnbull (Eds.), *Transitions to adult life for persons with mental retardation: Principles and practices* (pp. 293–311). Baltimore, MD: Paul H. Brookes.

Patton, J. R., Cronin, M. E., Polloway, E. A., Hutchinson, D., & Robinson, G. (1989). Curricular considerations: A life skills orientation. In G. A. Robinson, J. R. Patton, E. A. Polloway, & L. R. Sargent (Eds.), *Best practices in mild mental retardation* (pp. 21–38). Reston, VA: Division on Mental Retardation, Council for Exceptional Children.

Polloway, E. A., Patton, J. R., Epstein, M. H., & Smith, T. (1989). Comprehensive curriculum for students with mild handicaps. *Focus on Exceptional Children, 21*(8), 1–12.

Polloway, E. A., & Patton, J. R. (1993). *Strategies for teaching learners with special needs* (5th ed.). New York: Macmillan.

Polloway, E. A., Patton, J. R., Smith, J. D., & Roderique, T. (1991). Issues in program design for elementary students with mild retardation: Emphasis on curriculum development. *Education and Training in Mental Retardation, 26,* 142–150.

Roessler, R. (1991). A problem-solving approach to implementing career education. *Career Development for Exceptional Individuals, 14,* 59–66.

Samuels, S. J. (1984). Basic academic skills. In J. E. Ysseldyke (Ed.), *School psychology: The state of the art.* Minneapolis: National School Psychology Inservice Training Network, University of Minnesota.

Sands, D. J., Woosley, T., & Dunlap, W. R. (1985). *National Independent Living Skills Screening Instrument.* Tuscaloosa: The University of Alabama.

Smith, M. A., & Schloss, P. J. (1988). Teaching to transition. In P. J. Schloss, C. A. Hughes, & M. A. Smith (Eds.), *Community integration for persons with mental retardation* (pp. 1–16). Austin, TX: PRO-ED.

Spady, W. G. (1986). The emerging paradigm of organizational excellence: Success through planned adaptability. *Peabody Journal of Education, 63*(3), 46–64.

Spady, W. G., & Marshall, K. J. (1991). Beyond traditional outcome-based education. *Educational Leadership, 49*(2), 67–72.

Strickland, B. B., & Turnbull, A. P. (1990). *Developing and implementing individualized education programs* (3rd ed.). New York: Macmillan.

U.S. Office of Special Education Programs. (1992). *Fourteenth annual report to Congress on the implementation of the Education of the Handicapped Act.* Washington, DC: Office of Special Education and Rehabilitative Services, Department of Education.

Wagner, M. (1991). *Dropouts with disabilities: What do we know? What can we do?* Menlo Park, CA: SRI International.

White, W., Alley, G., Deshler, D., Schumaker, J., Warner, M., & Clark, F. (1982). Are there learning disabilities after high school? *Exceptional Children, 49,* 273–274.

Wiederholt, J. L., & Larsen, S. (1983). *Test of Practical Knowledge.* Austin, TX: PRO-ED.

Wood, J. (1992). *Adapting instruction for mainstreamed and at-risk students.* New York: Macmillan.

Woodward, D. M., & Peters, D. J. (1983). *The learning disabled adolescent: Learning success in content areas.* Rockville, MD: Aspen.

Zigmond, N., & Sansone, J. (1986). Designing a program for the learning disabled adolescent. *Remedial and Special Education, 7*(5), 13–17.

Materials List

MATERIAL ANALYSIS

One of the most time-consuming tasks for teachers is identifying and gathering materials for instruction. To help alleviate that cumbersome job for teachers of life skills, we have put together the following life skills materials list. **It comprises materials from selected publishers and is not considered to be comprehensive.** We offer it as a general source and a starting point for teachers. We encourage teachers who use this listing to write or call the publishers to obtain a recent catalog, as new materials are added constantly and older or outdated ones are removed. Those addresses and phone numbers can be found in Appendix B. We have not listed prices, which are subject to change. We also encourage teachers to build on this list as they find publications in their search for materials to meet life skills instructional needs.

The list is organized by the 23 subdomains identified in Table 2.2. Column one contains the name of the material. The publisher's three-letter code is in column two. The recommended age (if stated), the reading level (if stated), and the type of material (workbook, video, filmstrip, flash cards, etc.) can be found in columns three, four, and five, respectively. The codes for the publishers, age, and types of material follow this discussion. The age codes listed are recommendations found in the publishers' catalogs.

PUBLISHERS

Publisher Code	Publisher Name
ABN	Able Net, Inc.
ACT	Academic Therapy Publications
AGS	AGS
ASP	Aspen Publishers, Inc.
ATT	Attainment Company, Inc.
CDL	Cambridge Development Lab, Inc.
CEC	Council for Exceptional Children
CNV	The Conover Company
COM	ComputAbility Corporation
CON	Contemporary Books, Inc.
CSB	Communication Skill Builders
CUI	Cuisenaire Company
CUR	Curriculum Associates, Inc.
DJD	Don Johnston Development Equipment, Inc.
EAC	Educational Activities
EBS	EBSCO Curriculum Materials
EDI	Educational Design, Inc.
EDM	Edmark
EDT	EdITS
ENT	Entry Publishing, Inc.
EPR	Educational Press
ERE	Educational Resources
ESW	Exceptional Educational Software
FJA	Fearon/Janus/Quercus
GAM	Gamco Industries
GLO	Globe Book Company
HEL	Harvest Educational Labs
HIN	High Noon Books
JMS	James Stanfield Publishing Company
LCM	Lakeshore Curriculum Materials Company
LLS	Laureate Learning Systems, Inc.
LRS	Learning Resources Store
LSI	LinguiSystems, Inc.
MEM	Media Materials, Inc.
MGW	Magnetic Way
PCI	Programming Concepts, Inc.
PEK	Peekan Publications
PRO	PRO-ED, Inc.
PSE	Project Special Education
REP	Research Press

Publisher Code	Publisher Name
RPM	RPM Press, Inc.
SAD	Saddleback Educational, Inc.
SRA	SRA
STV	Steck-Vaughn
SUN	Sunburst Communications
SWE	Software for Education
THK	Thinking Publications
USG	U.S. Government Books
VGM	VGM Career Horizons

TYPES OF MATERIALS

A	Audiotapes
B	Book
CP	Comprehensive Program
DM	Duplication Master
F	Film
FC	Flash cards
FS	Filmstrip
G	Game
I	Infofile
K	Kit
M	Map
MN	Manipulative
P	Poster
PH	Pamphlet
RB	Resource Book
S	Slides
ST	Stamp
SW	Software
T	Test
TP	Transparency
TR	Teacher Resource
V	Video
W	Workbook

AGE LEVELS

EL	Elementary
MS	Middle School
JH	Junior High
HS	High School
AD	Adult

GENERAL JOB SKILLS

Material	Publisher	Age Level	Reading Level	Type
A Guide to Vocational Assessment	PRO	—	—	B
A Way to Work	ATT	HS	—	K
Applying for a Job	MEM	—	—	W
Attitude for Work	FJA	JH–HS	2.7	W
Basic Skills for Food Service Workers	HEL	HS–AD	—	V
Book 1: First Steps to Employability	EDI	MS–JH	3.0–5.0	W
Breaking Out	LLS	HS	—	V
Building Success in the Workplace	STV	AD	3.0–4.0	W
Buying with Sense	FJA	—	—	W
Career Awareness Plus	SAD	HS–AD	2.0–3.5	B
Career Box	FJA	JH–HS	3.5–5.0	F
Career Box Worksheets	FJA	JH–HS	3.5–5.0	W
Career Math Makes Sense	FJA	—	—	W
Career Skills	SAD	MS–AD	4.0–5.0	W/B
Career Words Data Disks	EBS	HS	—	SW
Career: Exploration & Decision	FJA	JH–HS	5.0–6.0	W
Classroom Cash	EDM	—	—	K
Coins Skills Curriculum, Revised	EDM	EL	—	TR
Communicate	THK	MS–HS	—	G
Communicate Expansion Cards	THK	MS–HS	—	G
Communication Skills	COM	MS–AD	4.0–5.0	SW
Communication Skills at Work: Customers	HEL	HS–AD	—	V
Communication Skills at Work: Supervisors	HEL	HS–AD	—	V
Competitive Job Finding Guide for Persons with Handicaps	PRO	HS–AD	—	B/W
COPSystem Career Briefs Kit	EDT	MS–AD	—	I
COPSystem Career Cluster Booklets	EDT	MS–AD	—	P
COPSystem Comprehensive Career Guidebook	EDT	—	—	B
COPSystem Occupational Cluster Charts	EDT	—	—	P
COPSystem Picture Inventory of Careers COPS-PIC	EDT	EL–AD	—	T
Daily Communication: Strategies for the Language Disordered Student	THK	MS–HS	—	B/DM
Decisions at Work	HEL	HS–AD	3.0–4.0	F/W
Developing Everyday Reading Skills, Books 1 and 2	EDI	—	2.0–4.0	W
Developing Functional English Skill Series: Letter Writing	MEM	MS–AD	—	W
Developing Functional English Skill Series: Writing for Your Life	MEM	MS–AD	—	W
Developing Your Job Search Skills	SAD	JH–HS	—	W

GENERAL JOB SKILLS (continued)

Material	Publisher	Age Level	Reading Level	Type
Directing Your Successful Job Search	HEL	HS–AD	—	V
Don't Be Fired!	FJA	JH–HS	2.5–4.0	W
Don't Call Us: We'll Call You	LCM	—	4.0–5.0	DM
Emerging Occupations Interest Inventory	ESW	HS–AD	—	T
Employability Skills Program	SAD	JH–AD	2.5–4.0	B
Employability Skills System	CNV	—	—	SW
English for the World of Work	MEM	MS–AD	—	B/W
Equal Employment Opportunity	MEM	—	—	W
Essential Life Skills Series	CSB	JH–AD	—	W
Exploring Measurement, Time, & Money	EDM	EL	—	SW
Filling Out Forms	FJA	HS	—	A/W
Filling Out Job Applications	ESW	HS–AD	3.0–4.0	SW
Finding a Job	FJA	JH–HS	3.0	W
First Jobs	EDI	MS–AD	—	V/FS
Forms	FJA	JH–HS	2.2–2.6	W
Forms in Your Future	GLO	—	—	W
Get Hired!	FJA	JH–HS	2.5–4.0	W
Get Set for Work	MEM	HS–AD	4.0	W
Get That Job	FJA	JH–HS	2.2	W
Getting a Job	EPR	JH–AD	5.0	W
Handbook of Career Planning for Special Needs Students	AGS	—	—	TR
Health Service Occupations	HEL	—	—	F/V
Hospital Jobs	FJA	JH–HS	2.0–3.5	W
Hospital Words	FJA	JH–HS	2.0–3.5	W
Hotel/Motel Jobs	FJA	JH–HS	2.0–3.5	W
Hotel/Motel Words	FJA	JH–HS	2.0–3.5	W
How Should I Do It	EPR	JH–AD	4.0	W
How to Complete Job Applications and Resumes	SRA	MS–HS	2.4–4.0	W
How to Get A Job and Keep It	STV	AD	5.0–6.0	W
How to Hold Your Job	PRO	HS–AD	3.0	B/W
How to Land a Better Job	VGM	—	—	B
How to Look Good to Employers	FJA	JH–HS	5.0	W
How to Use the Classified Ads	SRA	MS–HS	2.5–5.0	W
How to Use the Newspaper	SRA	MS–HS	2.5–5.0	W
How to Use the Telephone Book	SRA	MS–HS	2.5–5.0	W
How To Write 2: Forms and More	ENT	—	—	W
How to Write a Winning Resume	VGM	—	—	B
How to Write for Everyday Living Software	LCM	—	3.5–4.5	SW/CP
Interview Packet	PEK	—	—	B/W

GENERAL JOB SKILLS *(continued)*

Material	Publisher	Age Level	Reading Level	Type
Intro to the Business Office	ESW	—	—	SW
Introduction to Business Office	COM	—	—	SW
Introduction to Skills for School Success	CUR	MS–AD	—	V
Job Survival Skills	HEL	HS–AD	—	V
Job Applications & Other Forms	MEM	HS–AD	2.0–4.0	W
Job Attitudes: Assessment & Improvement	ESW	HS–AD	3.0–4.0	SW
Job Awareness Kit	MEM	MS–AD	4.0	K
Job Box	FJA	JH–HS	2.5–3.0	F
Job Box Key	SAD	JH–AD	2.5–3.0	B/DM
Job Box Worksheets	FJA	JH–HS	2.5–3.0	W
Job Club Counselor's Manual	PRO	AD	—	B
Job Interview	MEM	—	—	W
Job Interview PracticePak	EDM	—	—	K
Job Interview Skills	EDI	—	—	V
Job Readiness	COM	—	—	SW
Job Readiness Series	FJA	HS	—	SW
Job Readiness Skills	HEL	HS–AD	3.0–4.0	SW
Job Search	ESW	—	—	SW
Job Search Education	EDI	—	—	W
Job Seeking Skills	HEL	HS–AD	2.5–3.0	W
Job Success	HEL	HS–AD	3.0	SW
Job Success Series	COM	—	—	SW
Job Survival Skills	EDI	—	3.0–6.0	W
Jobs I Can Do	MEM	HS–AD	2.4	W
Jobs in Today's World	ESW	HS–AD	3.0–4.0	T
Keeping a Job	FJA	JH–HS	3.0	W
Kitchen Safety	HEL	HS–AD	—	V
Learn to Earn	MEM	HS–AD	2.0–4.0	W
Learning Activity Packets	CNV	—	—	SW
Letter Writing	EDI	—	low	W
Letters for Your Resume	ERE	—	—	SW
Life Skills Reading, Book 1	EDI	—	3.0–5.0	W
Life Skills Writing	EDI	—	3.0–5.0	W
Living on Your Own: An Independent Living Simulation	FJA	JH–HS	—	DM
Living Skills Series, Book 2: New Rights & Responsibilities	EDI	HS	—	W
Math for the Carpenter or Plumber or Health Care Worker	EAC	—	—	A/B
Me & Jobs	EDI	—	3.0–6.0	W
Me & Jobs Video	EDI	—	—	V/FS

GENERAL JOB SKILLS *(continued)*

Material	Publisher	Age Level	Reading Level	Type
Measure Up	FJA	EL–JH	2.7	W
Money Flashcards	EDM	—	—	FC/W
New Visions: Survival Skills	FJA	HS	—	K
Occupational Notebook	EDM	MS–HS	—	W
Occupational Outlook Handbook: 1990–1991	USG	—	—	TR
On My Own With Language	LSI	MS–HS	4.5–5.5	DM
On the Job	HEL	HS	4.0	V
Opportunity 2000: Creative Affirmative Action Strategies for a Changing Workforce	USG	—	—	B
Pacemaker Career Readers	FJA	JH–HS	2.0	W/A
People Working Today	EDM	MS–HS	2.0	B
Reading & Following Directions	FJA	JH–HS	2.0–3.5	W
Reading Want Ads	MEM	MS–AD	2.4	W
Ready to Work: Winning at the Job Game	CON	HS–AD	4.0–5.0	W
Real Life Employment Skills	LCM	—	4.5–6.0	W/B
Real Life Math	PRO	JH–HS	4.5–6.0	K
Reasoning Skills on the Job	CNV	HS–AD	3.5–5.0	SW
Responsibility & Independence Scales for Adolescents	SRA	MS–HS	—	T
Restaurant Jobs	FJA	JH–HS	2.0–3.5	W
Restaurant Words	FJA	JH–HS	2.0–3.5	W
Resume	ERE	—	—	SW
Resumes Made Easy	ESW	HS–AD	3.0–4.0	SW
Retail Trade Occupations	HEL	—	—	F/V
Serious Business	SRA	MS–HS	4.0–5.0	W
Social Perceptual Training for Community Living	EAC	—	—	K
Social Skills at Work	HEL	HS–AD	—	V
Social Skills on the Job	HEL	HS–AD	0–4.0	K
Sources of Job Information	MEM	—	—	W
Store Jobs	FJA	JH–HS	2.0–3.5	W
Store Words	FJA	JH–HS	2.0–3.5	W
Study Attitudes & Methods Survey SAMS	EDT	JH–AD	—	T
Success at Work	HEL	HS–AD	—	K
Successful Job Interviewing	ESW	HS–AD	3.0–4.0	SW
Survival Words	EBS	—	—	SW
The Amazing Adventures of Harvey Crumbaker	LCM	—	4.0–5.0	DM
The Career Ability Placement Survey	EDT	—	—	T
The Career Orientation Placement and Evaluation Survey	EDT	—	—	T
The Employability Inventory	FJA	HS	—	SW
The Job of Getting A Job	MEM	HS–AD	2.4	W

GENERAL JOB SKILLS *(continued)*

Material	Publisher	Age Level	Reading Level	Type
The World of Work Series	EDI	—	—	W/A
There's a Career for You in Home Economics	ESW	—	—	SW
Using Dollars & Sense	FJA	—	—	W
Using Phones and Phone Books	PEK	—	—	W
Using a Telephone	PRO	MS–AD	—	K
Using the Newspaper to Teach Basic Living Skills	FJA	HS	—	DM
Using the Newspaper to Teach Basic Living Skills	EBS	HS	3.0	DM
Vocational Curriculum for Developmentally Disabled Persons	PRO	—	—	B
Vocational Entry-Skills for Secondary Students	ACT	HS	—	W
Vocational Entry Skills for Secondary Students	ACT	HS	—	W
Vocational Training Curriculums for Special Needs Students	REP	—	—	B
Way to Work	FJA	JH–HS	2.3	W
What's Next	EPR	JH–AD	4.0	W
Work Habits and Attitudes	HEL	HS–AD	—	F
Work World	EAC	—	3.0	K/CP
Work-Wise: Tactics for Job Success	CON	HS–AD	6.0–8.0	W
Working 1	JMS	—	—	V
Working for a Living	HEL	HS–AD	—	V
Working in Daycare	HEL	—	—	F/V
Working in English	CON	HS–AD	—	W
Working in Home Health Care	HEL	—	—	F/V
World of Work	HEL	HS–AD	—	F
Would I Work With Me	HEL	HS–AD	—	V
Writing for a Reason	SAD	MS–HS	2.5	W/B
Writing for the World of Work	EDI	—	4.0–7.0	W
Writing Friendly Letters, Business Letters, & Resumes	FJA	HS	—	A/W
X4LD: How to Join the Job Club	ACT	HS	—	TR
Yes I Can . . . Get That Job	REP	—	—	K
Your First Job	ESW	HS–AD	4.0–5.0	SW
Your Paperchase to Employment	EBS	—	—	W
Your Personal Job Search Journal	PEK	—	—	W
Your Work Habits	ESW	HS–AD	4.0–5.0	SW

GENERAL EDUCATION/TRAINING CONSIDERATIONS

Material	Publisher	Age Level	Reading Level	Type
A Guide to Vocational Assessment	PRO	—	—	B
A Way to Work	ATT	HS	—	K
Academic Survival Tips for Student Athletes	LLS	—	—	A
Analogies	SAD	MS–HS	—	W
Around the World in However Many Days it Takes	LCM	—	4.0–5.0	DM
Basic Skills for Food Service Workers	HEL	HS–AD	—	V
Basic Skills/Study Techniques Program	LLS	—	—	K
Basic Study Skills	LCM	—	3.5–5.5	W
Book 3: Working for Yourself	EDI	MS–HS	3.0–5.0	W
Building Memory Skills	ESW	—	—	SW
Building Real Life English Skills	LCM	HS–AD	5.5–6.5	CP
Career Planning: Putting Your Skills to Work	HEL	HS–AD	—	V
Careers in Health Care	VGM	—	—	B
Careers in Science	VGM	—	—	B
Cause & Effect Games	CSB	HS–AD	—	CP
Classification & Organization Skills—Developmental	CUR	HS–AD	6.0	W
College Prep Course	MEM	HS–AD	9.0–12.0	W
Community Signs	COM	—	—	SW
Computer Assisted Writing	EAC	—	—	SW
Computer Test Preparation	LLS	HS–AD	—	SW
Dictionary Skills Practice	CUR	MS–AD	4.0	W
Dilemma	EAC	—	2.5	SW
Effective Reading	LLS	—	—	A/W
Employment Signs	ATT	—	—	SW
English for Everyday Living	SAD	MS–HS	4.5–5.5	B
Essential Life Skill Series	SAD	JH–AD	5.0	W/B
Everyday Science	LCM	—	5.0–5.5	B
Everything You Need to Know About Financial Aid	LLS	—	—	V
Filling Out Forms	FJA	HS	—	A/W
First Days on the Job	ESW	HS–AD	4.0–5.0	SW
Following Directions	ESW	—	—	SW
Following Directions—Advanced	CUR	HS–AD	6.0	W
Footsteps	PEK	—	—	K
Foundation of Library Skills Series	ERE	—	—	SW
General Mathematics Project	SAD	HS–AD	—	W
Getting Smarter	FJA	JH–HS	4.0–6.0	W
Handbook for Citizenship Kit	LCM	—	2.5–4.5	A/B
Hands On Measurement Program	LCM	—	4.0–5.0	K
How to Make the Right College Choice	LLS	—	—	V

GENERAL EDUCATION/TRAINING CONSIDERATIONS (continued)

Material	Publisher	Age Level	Reading Level	Type
How to Modify Voc Ed for Handicapped Students	LLS	—	—	TR
How to Prepare for College	VGM	—	—	B
How to Study	AGS	JH–SH	—	W
How to Succeed in College	LLS	—	—	V
How to Write a Winning Resume	VGM	—	—	B
How to Write for Everyday Living Software	LCM	—	3.5–4.5	SW/CP
I Dropped Out . . . The Series	EBS	—	—	V
I Hate School Survival Guide	LCM	—	6.5–7.5	B
Improving Your Study Skills	MEM	MS–AD	—	W
Information Signs	ATT	—	—	SW
Inside Strategies for the SAT	EDI	—	—	W
Instructional Facilities	MEM	—	—	W
Interesting Careers	EAC	—	4.0–5.0	K
Introduction to Skills for School Success	CUR	MS–AD	—	V
It's There, But You Can't See It	LCM	—	4.0–5.0	DM
Janus Job Application File	FJA	JH–HS	2.5–4.0	W
Janus Job Interview Pak	FJA	JH–HS	2.5–4.0	K
Janus Job Interview Guide	FJA	JH–HS	2.5–4.0	W
Janus Job Planner	FJA	JH–HS	2.5–4.0	W
Keeping At Risk Students in School	CNV	—	—	V
Know Your Body	PEK	—	—	W
Learning Improvement Series	FJA	JH–HS	3.5	SW
Learning Styles Inventory	CNV	—	—	SW
Listening & Notetaking	EAC	—	—	A/B
Living Math	PEK	JH–AD	2–4	I/TR
Look, Listen & Touch	ESW	—	—	SW
Making the Grade	SAD	JH–HS	—	W
Making the Grade	HEL	—	5.0	SW
Making the Grade	LLS	—	—	SW
Map Skills	ERE	—	—	SW
Mastering Writing Skills	LCM	—	5.0–6.0	W
Math Skill Pack	SAD	HS–AD	2.0–5.0	A
Mathematics for Consumers	MEM	MS–AD	—	K
Me & Jobs	EDI	—	3.0–6.0	W
Measure Up	FJA	EL–JH	2.7	W
Measuring Skills	HEL	—	—	K
Mind Games: Puzzles in Logic	SAD	MS–HS	—	W
Mind Your Manners—Social Success	JMS	—	—	V
New Reports	PEK	—	—	A/W

GENERAL EDUCATION/TRAINING CONSIDERATIONS *(continued)*

Material	Publisher	Age Level	Reading Level	Type
New Visions: Survival Skills	FJA	HS	—	K
Notetaking	PEK	—	—	K
Now You're Talking	EAC	—	—	K
Occumatics	PEK	—	—	W
Opportunities in Counseling & Development Careers	VGM	—	—	B
Opportunities in Data Processing Careers	VGM	—	—	B
Opportunities in Fire Protection Services	VGM	—	—	B
Opportunities in Human Resources Management Careers	VGM	—	—	B
Opportunities in Biotechnology Careers	VGM	—	—	B
Opportunities in Building Construction Trades	VGM	—	—	B
Opportunities in Fast Food Careers	VGM	—	—	B
Opportunities in Journalism Careers	VGM	—	—	B
Opportunities in Medical Technology Careers	VGM	—	—	B
Opportunities in Military Careers	VGM	—	—	B
Opportunities in Newspaper Publishing	VGM	—	—	B
Opportunities in Nursing Careers	VGM	—	—	B
Opportunities in Petroleum Careers	VGM	—	—	B
Opportunities in Property Management Careers	VGM	—	—	B
Opportunities in Purchasing Careers	VGM	—	—	B
Opportunities in Refrigeration and Air Conditioning Trades	VGM	—	—	B
Opportunities in Restaurant Careers	VGM	—	—	B
Opportunities in Social Science Careers	VGM	—	—	B
Opportunities in Teaching Careers	VGM	—	—	B
Opportunities in Telecommunications Careers	VGM	—	—	B
Programmed Study Technique and Study Habits Survey	AGS	JH–HS	—	W/T
Reading Between the Lines	SAD	HS	—	W
Ready, Set, Study: Building Study Skills	CON	HS–AD	4.0–6.0	W
Ready, Set, Study: Improving Study Skills	CON	HS–AD	6.0–8.0	W
Real Reference	EBS	—	—	I
Reasoning Skills on the Job	CNV	HS–AD	3.5–5.0	SW
Sack-Yourman Study Skills Program	MEM	HS–AD	9.0–12.0	K
Safety Signs	ATT	—	—	SW
Scholarships Today	LLS	—	—	SW
Self Awareness	VGM	—	—	B
Sign Language	FJA	JH–HS	2.0	W
Signs of Survival	THK	HS–AD	—	FC

GENERAL EDUCATION/TRAINING CONSIDERATIONS *(continued)*

Material	Publisher	Age Level	Reading Level	Type
Skills Pack	SAD	HS	2.0–4.0	A
Skills for Successful Test Taking	ESW	—	—	SW
Story Starters: Science	ERE	—	—	SW
Story Starters: Social Studies	ERE	—	—	SW
Strategies for Study	SAD	JH–HS	—	W
Strategies for Study	LCM	—	5.5–7.0	W/B
Study Aids	CON	HS–AD	—	W/B
Study and Work Habits	CNV	—	—	V
Study Skills	FJA	JH–HS	—	TP
Study Skills	HEL	JH–HS	—	V
Study Skills	ESW	—	—	SW
Study Skills & Strategies	MEM	HS–AD	—	W
Study Skills Book	AGS	GR4–6	—	W
Study Skills Series	SAD	MS–AD	4.5–7.5	W
Study Skills: Strategies & Practice	CUR	HS–AD	1.0–7.0	DM
Study To Succeed	ESW	—	—	SW
Study: A Key to Learning	FJA	JH–HS	—	A/W
Success in the Classroom	LLS	—	—	V
Survival Math Worktext	LCM	—	4.0–5.5	W/T
Survival Words	EBS	—	—	SW
Survival Words	ATT	—	—	SW
Tackling Teen Topics	CSB	HS	—	CP
Test Ready Mathematics	CUR	HS–AD	GR1.0–8.0	W
Test Ready Practice with Cloze	CUR	HS–AD	GR3.0–6.0	W
Test Ready Reading & Vocabulary	CUR	HS–AD	1.0–8.0	W
Test Taking Made Easy	ESW	—	—	SW
Test Taking Techniques	EAC	—	—	A/B
Tests of Applied Literacy Skills	FJA	—	—	T
The Dropout Prevention Program	LLS	—	—	K/TR
The Test Taker's Edge	SUN	MS–AD	—	SW
The Video Test Preparation Review Series	LLS	HS–AD	—	V
Tools for Transition Program	AGS	JH–SH	—	K
Typing	FJA	MS–HS	—	SW
United States Constitution	PEK	—	3.0	W
Vocational Math Series	LCM	—	4.0–7.5	W
What's Happening	PEK	—	—	W
Why Stay in School	EBS	—	—	V/DM
Working in English	CON	HS–AD	—	W
Writing Competency Practice	EAC	HS	—	B/DM

GENERAL EDUCATION/TRAINING CONSIDERATIONS *(continued)*

Material	Publisher	Age Level	Reading Level	Type
Writing for Competency	LCM	—	5.5–7.0	W
Writing Makes Sense	LCM	—	4.0–4.5	W
Your Personal Habits	ESW	HS–AD	4.0–5.0	SW
Your State and Its Constitution	PEK	—	—	W

EMPLOYMENT SETTING

Material	Publisher	Age Level	Reading Level	Type
A Good Worker	MEM	MS–AD	2.0–4.0	W
A Guide to Vocational Assessment	PRO	—	—	B
A Way to Work	ATT	HS	—	K
A Week in the Life of . . .	ENT	—	5.0	SW
Active Listening Program	THK	HS–AD	—	K
Adjusting to a New Boss	EPR	JH–AD	4.0	W
Applied Vocational Math	EBS	—	—	K
Attitude for Work	FJA	JH–HS	2.7	W
Attitudes & Habits in Everyday Living	EDI	MS–AD	—	V/FS
Book 3: Working for Yourself	EDI	MS–HS	3.0–5.0	W
Building Real Life English Skills	LCM	HS–AD	5.5–6.5	CP
Building Success in the Workplace	STV	AD	3.0–4.0	W
Career Awareness Plus	SAD	HS–AD	2.0–3.5	B
Career Skills	SAD	MS–AD	4.0–5.0	W/B
Career-Life Skills Packs	SAD	HS	2.5–4.0	K
Clock & Calendar Skills	EBS	MS–HS	3.0–4.0	DM
Communicating on the Job	EDI	—	—	V/FS
Communication Skills Series	SAD	AD	2.6–2.8	B/W
Community Signs	COM	—	—	SW
Computerized Training Systems	CNV	—	—	SW
Computers and the World of Work	EDI	—	—	V
Consideration for Co-Workers Rights	EPR	JH–AD	4.0	W
Consumer Math	EAC	—	—	K
Consumer Skills	SAD	—	3.0	W
Daily Communication: Strategies for the Language Disordered Adolescent	THK	MS–HS	—	B/DM
Developing Your Job Search Skills	SAD	JH–HS	—	W
Don't Be Fired!	FJA	JH–HS	2.5–4.0	W
Done on Time	EPR	JH–AD	<4.0	WB
Emerging Occupations Interest Inventory	ESW	HS–AD	—	T
Employability Skills Program	SAD	JH–AD	2.5–4.0	B
Employers & Child Care	USG	—	—	B
Employment Signs	ATT	—	—	SW
English for the World of Work	MEM	MS–AD	—	B/W
English on the Job	CNV	—	—	SW
English Survival Series	SAD	MS–AD	2.0–5.0	W
Equal Employment Opportunity	MEM	—	—	W
Essential Life Skill Series	SAD	JH–AD	5.0	W/B
Everyday English	SAD	JH–AD	—	W
Filling Out Job Applications	ESW	HS–AD	3.0–4.0	SW

EMPLOYMENT SETTING *(continued)*

Material	Publisher	Age Level	Reading Level	Type
Finding a Job	FJA	JH–HS	3.0	W
First Days on the Job	ESW	HS–AD	4.0–5.0	SW
First Jobs	EDI	MS–AD	—	V/FS
General Mathematics Project	SAD	HS–AD	—	W
Get Hired!	FJA	JH–HS	2.5–4.0	W
Get That Job	FJA	JH–HS	2.2	W
Good Grooming Habits	EPR	JH–AD	<4.0	W
Good Work Habits	MEM	HS–AD	2.0–4.0	W
Help, Please	EPR	JH–AD	4.0	W
Hospital Jobs	FJA	JH–HS	2.0–3.5	W
Hospital Words	FJA	JH–HS	2.0–3.5	W
Hotel/Motel Jobs	FJA	JH–HS	2.0–3.5	W
Hotel/Motel Words	FJA	JH–HS	2.0–3.5	W
How Does It Work	EPR	JH–AD	4.0	W
How to Get A Job and Keep It	STV	AD	5.0–6.0	W
How to Look Good to Employers	FJA	JH–HS	5.0	W
How to Understand and Manage Your Time	SRA	MS–HS	2.5–5.0	W
Information Signs	ATT	—	—	SW
Introduction to Skills for School Success	CUR	MS–AD	—	V
Janus Job Application File	FJA	JH–HS	2.5–4.0	W
Janus Job Interview Pak	FJA	JH–HS	2.5–4.0	K
Janus Job Interview Guide	JFA	JH–HS	2.5–4.0	W
Janus Job Planner	FJA	JH–HS	2.5–4.0	W
Job Accomodation Handbook	REP	—	—	TR
Job Attitudes	FJA	HS	—	A/FS
Job Attitudes and Habits	EDI	MS–AD	—	V/FS
Job Attitudes Video Cassettes	FJA	HS	—	V
Job Attitudes: Assessment & Improvement	ESW	HS–AD	3.0–4.0	SW
Job Awareness Kit	MEM	MS–AD	4.0	K
Job Challenges	MEM	HS–AD	2.0–4.0	W
Job Coaching Kit	RPM	—	—	K
Job Performance	MEM	—	—	W
Job Readiness Series	FJA	HS	—	SW
Job Readiness Skills	HEL	HS–AD	3.0–4.0	SW
Job Search	ESW	—	—	SW
Job Search Education	EDI	—	—	W
Job Success	HEL	HS–AD	3.0	SW
Job Survival Skills	EDI	—	3.0–6.0	W
Jobs in Today's World	ESW	HS–AD	3.0–4.0	T
Keep Calm	EPR	JH–AD	4.0	W

EMPLOYMENT SETTING (continued)

Material	Publisher	Age Level	Reading Level	Type
Keeping a Job	FJA	JH–HS	3.0	W
Late for Work	EPR	JH–AD	4.0	W
Learn to Earn	MEM	HS–AD	2.0–4.0	W
Leaving Early	EPR	JH–AD	<4.0	W
Let's Calculate Activities	LCM	—	3.0–4.0	DM
Life Skills Attitudes in Everyday Living	EDI	MS–AD	3.0–5.0	W
Life Skills Attitudes on the Job	EDI	MS–AD	3.0–5.0	W
Life Skills Listening	EDI	MS–AD	2.0–4.0	A/W
Life Skills Writing	EDI	—	3.0–5.0	W
Making the Best Use of Time	EPR	JH–AD	4.0	W
Math for Employment	EDI	MS–AD	3.0–4.0	W
Math for Everyday Living	EAC	—	4.0–6.0	SW
Math for Everyday Living	EAC	MS–AD	—	A/B
Math for Food Service Occupations	EDI	MS–AD	3.0–4.0	W
Math for the World of Work	EDI	MS–AD	4.0–6.0	W
Math Map Trip	EAC	EL	—	K
Math on the Job	CNV	—	—	SW
Math Skill Pack	SAD	HS–AD	2.0–5.0	A
Math Survival: Wages/Salaries/Paychecks	MEM	MS–HS	1.3	B
Math Survival: Wages/Salaries/Paychecks	MEM	MS–HS	1.3	W
Math Survival: Weekly Time Cards	MEM	MS–HS	1.3	W
May I Try It	EPR	JH–AD	<4.0	W
Medical Words	ATT	—	—	SW
Neatness Counts	EPR	JH–AD	<4.0	W
New Visions: Survival Skills	FJA	HS	—	K
Occupational Outlook Handbook: 1990–1991	USG	—	—	TR
On-the-Job Training	EPR	HS	5.0–6.0	W
Payday! Managing Your Paycheck	FJA	JH–HS	2.5–4.0	W
Practicing Occupational Reading Skills: Automotive	STV	AD	5.0–6.0	W
Practicing Occupational Reading Skills: Business	STV	AD	5.0–6.0	W
Practicing Occupational Reading Skills: Carpentry	STV	AD	5.0–6.0	W
Practicing Occupational Reading Skills: Electronics	STV	AD	5.0–6.0	W
Practicing Occupational Reading Skills: Health Care	STV	AD	5.0–6.0	W
Practicing Occupational Reading Skills: Machine Trades	STV	AD	5.0–6.0	W
Respect for Property	EPR	JH–AD	4.0	WB
Restaurant Jobs	FJA	JH–HS	2.0–3.5	W
Restaurant Words	FJA	JH–HS	2.0–3.5	W

EMPLOYMENT SETTING (continued)

Material	Publisher	Age Level	Reading Level	Type
Resumes Made Easy	ESW	HS–AD	3.0–4.0	SW
Role Playing Situations	EPR	HS	5.0–6.0	I
Safety Signs	ATT	—	—	SW
Safety Training Kit	REP	—	—	K
Signs of Survival	THK	HS–AD	—	FC
Skill Packs	SAD	HS	2.0–4.0	A
Skills for Job Success	EPR	JH–AD	4.0	W/CP
Social Competence and Employability Skills Curriculum	ASP	HS	—	TR
Social Competence for Workers with Developmental Disabilities	EDM	—	—	TR
Social Skill Strategies	THK	MS–HS	6.0–7.0	B/DM
Social Skills on the Job/Career & Social Skills	CNV	—	—	SW
Starting Your New Job	EPR	JH–AD	5.0	W
Store Jobs	FJA	JH–HS	2.0–3.5	W
Store Words	FJA	JH–HS	2.0–3.5	W
Strategies for Solving Math Word Problems	EDI	MS–AD	3.0–4.0	W
Study Smart	THK	MS–HS	—	G
Study Smart Expansion Cards	THK	MS–HS	—	G
Success at Work	HEL	HS–AD	—	K
Successful Job Interviewing	ESW	HS–AD	3.0–4.0	SW
Survival Vocabulary	SAD	JH–AD	2.0–4.0	B/W
Survival Words	ATT	—	—	SW
Take Time	PRO	—	—	TR
Taking a Break	EPR	JH–AD	<4.0	W
Tele-Trainer	EDM	MS–HS	—	K
Telephone Skills	EBS	MS–HS	—	K
The Employability Inventory	FJA	HS	—	SW
The Guide to Basic Skills Jobs, Volume 1	REP	—	—	RB
The Job Book	MEM	HS–AD	2.4	W
The Payoff	SRA	MS/HS	4.0–5.0	W
The Time Is Now	PRO	EL–AD	1.0	W
The World of Work	EBS	EL–JH	—	K
The World of Work Series	EDI	—	—	W/A
There's a Career for You in Home Economics	ESW	—	—	SW
Time & Telling Time	FJA	EL–JH	2.9	W
Too Much Talking	EPR	JH–AD	4.0	W
Transfer Activities: Thinking Skill Vocabulary Development	THK	MS–HS	—	B/DM
Transportation Signs	ATT	—	—	SW

EMPLOYMENT SETTING *(continued)*

Material	Publisher	Age Level	Reading Level	Type
Using a Telephone	PRO	MS–AD	—	K
Using Want Ads	FJA	JH–HS	2.0–3.5	W
Vocabulary Building	SAD	MS–HS	—	DM
Vocabulary for the World of Work Books 1&2	EDI	—	—	W
Way to Work	FJA	JH–HS	2.3	W
What Should I Do	EPR	JH–AD	4.0	W
What You Should Know About Avoiding Rape and Sexual Assault	USG	—	—	P
What's the Proper Way	EPR	JH–AD	4.0	W
Which Tools to Use	EPR	JH–AD	<4.0	W
Which Way is Right	EPR	JH–AD	<4.0	W
Who Can Help	EPR	JH–AD	4.0	W
Will You Do Me a Favor	EPR	JH–AD	4.0	W
Work Behavior Training Program	EBS	—	—	K
Work Force Literacy Skills for Jobs 2000, Books 1&2	EDI	MS–AD	5.0–8.0	W
Work World	EAC	—	3.0	K/CP
Work-Wise: Tactics for Job Success	CON	HS–AD	6.0–8.0	W
Working I	JMS	—	—	V
Working II	JMS	—	—	V/T
Working in English	CON	HS–AD	—	W
Working Makes Sense	LCM	—	3.5–4.5	W
Working Too Slowly	EPR	JH–AD	4.0	W
Working with Others	MEM	JH–AD	5.0	W
Workplace Posters	EBS	—	—	P
World of Work	HEL	HS–AD	—	F
Would I Work With Me	HEL	HS–AD	—	V
Writing for the World of Work	EDI	—	4.0–7.0	W
Workplace Skills	PCI	—	—	G
Yes I Can . . . Do the Job Right	REP	—	—	K
Yes I Can . . . Work with People	REP	—	—	K
You & Your New Job Series	EDI	—	—	V
Your First Job	ESW	HS–AD	4.0–5.0	SW
Your Personal Habits	ESW	HS–AD	4.0–5.0	SW
Your Work Habits	ESW	HS–AD	4.0–5.0	SW

CAREER REFINEMENT AND RE-EVALUATION

Material	Publisher	Age Level	Reading Level	Type
9–5 Series	HIN	MS–HS	3.0	B
Applied Vocational Math	EBS	—	—	K
Book 1: First Steps to Employability	EDI	MS–JH	3.0–5.0	W
Book 2: Working in Community Service	EDI	MS–HS	3.0–5.0	W
Breaking Out	LLS	HS	—	V
Career Assessment Inventories: For the Learning Disabled	ACT	EL–AD	—	T
Career Awareness Plus	SAD	HS–AD	2.0–3.5	B
Career Box	FJA	JH–HS	3.5–5.0	F
Career Box Worksheets	FJA	JH–HS	3.5–5.0	W
Career Education: A Curriculum Manual for Students with Handicaps	ASP	—	—	TR
Career Exploration Field Trips	EDI	MS–AD	—	V
Career Interest	LCM	—	3.5–4.5	SW
Career Options for Women	LLS	—	—	B
Career Planning System	CNV	—	—	SW
Career Preparation	ENT	—	—	SW
Career Readers	SAD	JH–AD	2.0	B
Career Skills	SAD	MS–AD	4.0–5.0	W/B
Career Words Data Disks	EBS	HS	—	SW
Career, Education, Life Options	EDI	—	—	V
Career-Life Skills Packs	SAD	HS	2.5–4.0	K
Career: Exploration & Decision	FJA	JH–HS	5.0–6.0	W
Careers in Health Care	VGM	—	—	B
Careers in Science	VGM	—	—	B
Careers that Count	LCM	—	6.0–7.0	FC
Choices and Challenges in Your Future	LCM	—	5.5–7.0	W/B
Competitive Job Finding Guide for Persons with Handicaps	PRO	HS–AD	—	B/W
Computers and the World of Work	EDI	—	—	V
COPSystem Career Briefs Kit	EDT	MS–AD	—	I
COPSystem Career Cluster Booklets	EDT	MS–AD	—	P
COPSystem Comprehensive Career Guidebook	EDT	—	—	B
COPSystem Occupational Cluster Charts	EDT	—	—	P
COPSystem Picture Inventory of Careers (COPS-PIC)	EDT	EL–AD	—	T
Dictionary of Occupational Titles	USG	—	—	B
Emerging Occupations Interest Inventory	COM	—	—	T/SW
Essential Life Skills Series	CSB	JH–AD	—	W
Exploring Careers	EDI	MS–AD	—	DM

CAREER REFINEMENT AND RE-EVALUATION *(continued)*

Material	Publisher	Age Level	Reading Level	Type
Finding a Job	FJA	JH–HS	3.0	W
First Jobs	EDI	MS–AD	—	V/FS
Get Hired!	FJA	JH–HS	2.5–4.0	W
Get That Job	FJA	JH–HS	2.2	W
Group Interest Sort	CNV	—	—	SW/T
Handbook of Career Planning for Special Needs Students	AGS	—	—	TR
Handbook of Occupational Groups & Series	USG	—	—	B
Health Service Occupations	HEL	—	—	F/V
Hospital Jobs	FJA	JH–HS	2.0–3.5	W
Hospital Words	FJA	JH–HS	2.0–3.5	W
Hotel/Motel Jobs	FJA	JH–HS	2.0–3.5	W
Hotel/Motel Words	FJA	JH–HS	2.0–3.5	W
INFO Job	SAD	JH–HS	—	B
Interesting Careers	EAC	—	4.0–5.0	K
Janus Job Application File	FJA	JH–HS	2.5–4.0	W
Janus Job Interview Pak	FJA	JH–HS	2.5–4.0	K
Janus Job Interview Guide	FJA	JH–HS	2.5–4.0	W
Janus Job Planner	FJA	JH–HS	2.5–4.0	W
Job Box	FJA	JH–HS	2.5–3.0	F
Job Box Key	SAD	JH–AD	2.5–3.0	B/DM
Job Box Worksheets	FJA	JH–HS	2.5–3.0	W
Job Outlook	HEL	—	—	F
Job Tips	SAD	JH–AD	2.7	B
Job Tips	LLS	—	—	P
Job Tips Library	LCM	—	2.5–4.0	B
Jobs I Can Do	MEM	HS–AD	2.4	W
Jobs in Today's World	COM	—	—	SW
Learn to Earn	MEM	HS–AD	2.0–4.0	W
Learning Improvement Series	FJA	JH–HS	3.5	SW
Making Change	EBS	MS–SH	—	SW
Math for Food Service Occupations	EDI	MS–AD	3.0–4.0	W
Mathematics Workshop: Exploring Careers	GLO	—	—	W
Me & Jobs Video	EDI	—	—	V/FS
Me & My Future	EDI	MS–HS	5.0–8.0	W
Microcomputer Evaluation of Career Areas	CNV	—	—	SW
Newspaper Literacy	EAC	—	—	SW/CP
Occupational Outlook Handbook: 1990–1991	USG	—	—	TR
Opportunities in Counseling & Development Careers	VGM	—	—	B

CAREER REFINEMENT AND RE-EVALUATION *(continued)*

Material	Publisher	Age Level	Reading Level	Type
Opportunities in Data Processing Careers	VGM	—	—	B
Opportunities in Fire Protection Services	VGM	—	—	B
Opportunities in Human Resources Management Careers	VGM	—	—	B
Opportunities in Biotechnology Careers	VGM	—	—	B
Opportunities in Building Construction Trades	VGM	—	—	B
Opportunities in Fast Food Careers	VGM	—	—	B
Opportunities in Journalism Careers	VGM	—	—	B
Opportunities in Medical Technology Careers	VGM	—	—	B
Opportunities in Military Careers	VGM	—	—	B
Opportunities in Newspaper Publishing	VGM	—	—	B
Opportunities in Nursing Careers	VGM	—	—	B
Opportunities in Petroleum Careers	VGM	—	—	B
Opportunities in Property Management Careers	VGM	—	—	B
Opportunities in Purchasing Careers	VGM	—	—	B
Opportunities in Refrigeration and Air Conditioning Trades	VGM	—	—	B
Opportunities in Restaurant Careers	VGM	—	—	B
Opportunities in Social Science Careers	VGM	—	—	B
Opportunities in Teaching Careers	VGM	—	—	B
Opportunities in Telecommunications Careers	VGM	—	—	B
Outdoor Occupations	HEL	—	—	F
Pacemaker Career Readers	FJA	JH–HS	2.0	W/A
People Working Today	EDM	MS–HS	2.0	B
Practicing Occupational Reading Skills: Automotive	STV	AD	5.0–6.0	W
Practicing Occupational Reading Skills: Business	STV	AD	5.0–6.0	W
Practicing Occupational Reading Skills: Carpentry	STV	AD	5.0–6.0	W
Practicing Occupational Reading Skills: Electronics	STV	AD	5.0–6.0	W
Practicing Occupational Reading Skills: Health Care	STV	AD	5.0–6.0	W
Practicing Occupational Reading Skills: Machine Trades	STV	AD	5.0–6.0	W
Ready to Work: Winning at the Job Game	CON	HS–AD	4.0–5.0	W
Real Life Math	PRO	JH–HS	4.5–6.0	K
Real Reading	EBS	MS–HS	—	I
Restaurant Jobs	FJA	JH–HS	2.0–3.5	W
Restaurant Occupations	HEL	—	—	F
Restaurant Words	FJA	JH–HS	2.0–3.5	W
Retail Trade Occupations	HEL	—	—	F/V
Self Awareness	VGM	—	—	B
Social Skills on the Job	HEL	HS–AD	0–4.0	K

CAREER REFINEMENT AND RE-EVALUATION *(continued)*

Material	Publisher	Age Level	Reading Level	Type
Sources of Job Information	MEM	—	—	W
Specially Produced for Special Ed	EDI	—	—	FS
Store Jobs	FJA	JH–HS	2.0–3.5	W
Store Words	FJA	JH–HS	2.0–3.5	W
Study Attitudes & Methods Survey SAMS	EDT	JH–AD	—	T
The 9–5 Series	ENT	MS–HS	3.0–4.0	B
The Career Builders Video Series	EDI	—	—	V
The Career Search Programs	LLS	—	—	K
The COPS Interest Inventory	EDT	—	—	T
The Guide for Occupational Exploration	AGS	—	—	RB
The Harrington O'Shea Career Decision-Making System	AGS	HS–AD	—	T
The Info-job Resource Center	LCM	—	4.5–5.5	B
The Job Book	MEM	HS–AD	2.4	W
The Right Job	SUN	MS–AD	—	SW
The Woman Entrepreneur: Do You Have What It Takes?	LLS	—	—	V
The World of Work	EBS	EL–JH	—	K
Vocational Curriculum for Developmentally Disabled Persons	PRO	—	—	B
Vocational Readers	SAD	JH–AD	2.0	B
Vocational Training Curriculums for Special Needs Students	REP	—	—	B
Women in Non-Traditional Occupations	LLS	—	—	FS/V
Work a Day America	EAC	—	—	V
Worker Trait Group Guide	AGS	—	—	RB
Working in Daycare	HEL	—	—	F/V
Working in Home Health Care	HEL	—	—	F/V
Working with Computers	HEL	—	—	F
Working with Others	MEM	JH–AD	5.0	W
You and Your Career	MEM	—	—	W
You Are . . . . Series	HIN	MS–HS	4.0–5.0	B/W
You Decide Career Adventures	LCM	—	5.0–5.5	B
Pacemaker Vocational Readers	FJA	JH–HS	2.0	W/A

HOME MANAGEMENT

Material	Publisher	Age Level	Reading Level	Type
A Good Citizen at Home	MEM	MS–AD	2.0–4.0	W
A Special Picture Cookbook	PRO	EL	—	B
Adaptable Housing: Marketable Accessible Housing for Everyone	USG	—	—	B
Affordable Housing Through Energy Conservation	USG	—	—	B/SW
American Holidays	LCM	—	3.7–4.5	B
An Illustrated Guide to Electrical Safety	USG	—	—	B
Appliances	MEM	MS–AD	2.4	W
As the Year Passes	PEK	—	—	B
Baby Sitting	LLS	MS–HS	—	V
Bake & Taste	CDL	GR1–9	—	SW
Basic Cooking & Nutrition for Special Students	EBS	JH–HS	—	B/DM
Basic Electricity	USG	—	—	B
Basic Sewing	FJA	JH–HS	2.0–3.5	W
Be Ad-Wise	FJA	JH–HS	2.5	W
Be Your Own Plumber	LLS	—	—	V
Being with Housemates, Part 1 & 2	JMS	—	—	V
Body & Fender Parts	LLS	—	—	V
Budgeting	FJA	JH–HS	2.2–2.6	W
Buyer Beware	ESW	—	—	SW
Buying & Caring for Clothes	FJA	JH–HS	2.0–3.5	W
Buying a Home	MEM	—	—	W
Career-Life Skills Packs	SAD	HS	2.5–4.0	K
Caring for Your Car	FJA	JH–HS	2.5–4.0	W
Clock & Calendar Skills	EBS	MS–HS	3.0–4.0	DM
Community Skills	PCI	—	—	G
Complete Guide to Home Canning	USG	—	—	B
Computer & the World of Work	EDI	—	—	V
Conserving Energy in the Home	MEM	—	—	W
Consumer Matter	EAC	—	—	K
Consumer Skills	SAD	—	3.0	W
Consumer Skills, Math and Economics	SAD	JH–AD	2.5–3.0	W
Cooking	MEM	MS–AD	2.4	W
Cooking Class	PCI	—	—	G
Coping with Conversions	LCM	—	4.0–5.0	DM
Crash	PEK	—	—	G
Crime Prevention in the Home	LLS	—	—	V
Developing Everyday Reading Skills, Books 1 & 2	EDI	—	2.0–4.0	W
Dietary Guidelines for Americans	USG	—	—	B

HOME MANAGEMENT *(continued)*

Material	Publisher	Age Level	Reading Level	Type
Eating Better When Eating Out Using the Dietary Guidelines	USG	—	—	B
Eating Right	FJA	JH–HS	3.5–4.0	W
Emergency	FJA	HS	3.0–4.0	W
Employability Skills Program	SAD	JH–AD	2.5–4.0	B
Energy Conservation—Technical Information Guide, Volume 3, Residential Buildings	USG	—	—	B
English for Everyday Living	FJA	MS–HS	—	DM
Enjoying the Newspaper	EDI	MS–AD	—	W
Everyday Consumer English	LCM	—	4.5–6.0	B
Exploring Measurement, Time, & Money	EDM	EL	—	SW
First Aid	MEM	—	—	W
First Aid & Home Safety	FJA	MS–HS	3.5–5.0	W
Fixing Your Car	LCM	—	3.0–5.0	W
Food & Nutrition	EDI	JH–AD	3.0–6.0	W
Food & Nutrition	EDM	—	2.0–2.8	K
Food Chains	ESW	EL	—	SW
Food for Thought	SUN	MS–AD	—	SW
Food Labels	ESW	—	—	SW
Food/Housing/Clothing/Cooking	EDI	MS–AD	—	V/FS
Forecasting the Weather	ESW	EL	—	SW
Forms	FJA	JH–HS	2.2–2.6	W
Getting Ready to Cook	FJA	—	—	W
Haircutting at Home	LLS	—	—	V
Hands-On Measurement Program	LCM	—	4.0–5.0	K
Healthy Meal Planning	ESW	—	—	V
Healthy Meal Planning Away from Home	ESW	—	—	V
Home & School Cooperation	MEM	—	—	W
Home Cooking	ATT	—	—	K
Home Maintenance	MEM	—	—	W
Home Video System Maintenance	LLS	—	—	V
House-A-Fire	COM	—	—	SW
How to Buy a Home with Nothing Down	LLS	—	—	V
How to Care for Your Lawn	LLS	—	—	V
How to Design & Build a Vegetable Garden	LLS	—	—	V
How to Design a Flower Garden	LLS	—	—	V
How to Grow & Cook Herbs	LLS	—	—	V
How to Grow & Nurture Seedlings	LLS	—	—	V
How to Grow Cool-Weather Vegetables	LLS	—	—	V
How to Grow Flowers	LLS	—	—	V

HOME MANAGEMENT (continued)

Material	Publisher	Age Level	Reading Level	Type
How to Grow Healthy Houseplants	LLS	—	—	V
How to Grow Plants in a Greenhouse	LLS	—	—	V
How to Grow Plants in Sunspaces	LLS	—	—	V
How to Grow Roses	LLS	—	—	V
How to Grow Warm-Weather Vegetables	LLS	—	—	V
How to Manage Your Personal Affairs	SRA	MS–HS	2.4–4.0	W
How to Understand & Manage Your Time	SRA	MS–HS	2.5–5.0	W
How to Use Measurements	SRA	MS–HS	2.5–5.0	W
How to Use the Classified Ads	SRA	MS–HS	2.5–5.0	W
How to Use the Newspaper	SRA	MS–HS	2.5–5.0	W
How to Use the Telephone Book	SRA	MS–HS	2.5–5.0	W
How To Write 1: From Lists to Letters	ENT	—	—	W
In the Driver's Seat	PEK	—	3.0	K
Information Signs	ATT	—	—	SW
Investigating Electricity Set	CUI	GR5–9	—	K
Keeping House	ATT	—	—	K
Kitchen Measures	EDM	—	—	F/A
Learning First Aid	MEM	MS–AD	—	W
Let's Calculate Activities	LCM	—	3.0–4.0	DM
Letter Writing	EDI	NS	low	W
Life Coping Skills Series: Facts & Sources	STV	MS–JH	2.0–4.0	W
Life Coping Skills Series: Forms & Messages	STV	MS–JH	2.0–4.0	W
Life Coping Skills Series: Signs & Labels	STV	MS–JH	2.0–4.0	W
Life Skills Mathematics	MEM	MS–AD	—	K
Life Skills Reading Book 1	EDI	—	3.0–5.0	W
Life Skills Writing	EDI	—	3.0–5.0	W
Living Alone	COM	HS–AD	3.0–4.0	SW
Living In the U.S.A.	SAD	JH–AD	—	B/W
Living on Your Own: An Independent Living Simulation	FJA	JH–HS	—	DM
Look 'n Cook	ATT	—	—	K
Looking Good Key	PCI	—	—	G
Making Bag Lunches, Snacks, and Desserts Using the Dietary Guidelines	USG	—	—	B
Mark Your Calendar	FJA	EL–HS	2.7	W
Math for Everyday Living	SAD	JH–HS	4.5–5.0	B
Mathematics in Daily Living	LCM	—	4.0–6.0	W
Measure Up	FJA	EL–JH	2.7	W
Measuring for Cooking	FJA	JH–HS	2.0–3.5	W
Measuring Skills	HEL	—	—	K

HOME MANAGEMENT *(continued)*

Material	Publisher	Age Level	Reading Level	Type
Modern Consumer Education	EDI	—	—	W/A
Money Matters Guides	SAD	MS–AD	2.5	W
Money Matters	SRA	—	—	WB
Money Matters	ESW	EL–AD	2.0	SW
More for Your Money	FJA	JH–HS	2.5	W
Mr. & Ms.	FJA	HS	3.0–4.0	W
My House: Language Activities of Daily Living	LLS	—	—	SW
Newspaper Literacy	EAC	—	—	SW/CP
Number Power	CON	HS–AD	—	W
Number Sense	CON	HS–AD	—	W
Nutrition in the Home	MEM	—	—	W
Oil Change, Filters, & Lube	LLS	—	—	V
On My Own at Home	LSI	MS–HS	5.5–6.5	DM
On My Own With Language	LSI	MS–HS	4.5–5.5	DM
Owning a Car	FJA	JH–HS	2.2–2.5	W
Paying With Promises	FJA	JH–HS	2.2–2.6	W
Peggy's Picture Cookbook	MEM	MS–HS	—	B
Plan Your Day	ATT	—	—	K
Planning for Your Own Apartment	FJA	JH–HS	3.0	W
Planning Healthy Meals	FJA	JH–HS	2.0–3.5	W
Planning Meals & Shopping	FJA	—	—	W
Plant Propagation Kit	CUI	GR5–9	—	K
Preparing Foods & Planning Menus Using the Dietary Guidelines	USG	—	—	B
Professional Tips for Easy Wallpapering	LLS	—	—	V
Reading & Following Recipes	FJA	JH–HS	2.0–3.5	W
Reading for Successful Living	FJA	JH–HS	—	SW
Real Facts: The Truth About Drugs	MEM	MS–AD	—	W
Real Life Reading: Food	MEM	MS–AD	2.4	W
Real Life Reading: Medicine	MEM	MS–AD	2.4	W
Real Life Reading: Shops & Services	MEM	MS–AD	2.4	W
Real Life Writing Skills	LCM	—	4.0–5.0	W
Real Numbers	CON	HS–AD	—	W
Renting	MEM	—	—	W
Replacing Exhaust Systems	LLS	—	—	V
Replacing Shocks and Struts	LLS	—	—	V
Responsibility and Independence Scales for Adolescents	SRA	MS–HS	—	T
Safe Living Reading Series	EAC	HS	2.5	K
Safety Signs	ATT	—	—	SW

HOME MANAGEMENT *(continued)*

Material	Publisher	Age Level	Reading Level	Type
Safety Training Kit	REP	—	—	K
Select-A-Meal	ATT	—	—	K
Sharing an Apartment	FJA	JH–HS	2.5–4.0	W
Shopping for Food and Making Meals in Minutes Using the Dietary Guidelines	USG	—	—	B
Simple Cooking	EDM	—	—	B
Solar Greenhouses & Sunspaces: Lessons Learned	USG	—	—	B
Special Picture Cookbook	PRO	—	—	B
Staying Healthy	FJA	MS–HS	3.5–5.0	W
Step Write Up! Writing Letters	ENT	—	—	SW
Survival Math	SAD	JH–AD	2.0–4.0	DM/A
Survival Math Skills	LCM	—	4.5–5.5	W
Survival Vocabulary	EBS	—	—	DM
Survival Words	ATT	—	—	SW
Take Time	PRO	—	—	TR
Taking Care of Yourself	FJA	MS–HS	2.3–3.0	W
The Amazing Adventures of Harvey Crumbaker	LCM	—	4.0–5.0	DM
The Backyard Mechanic Set, Volumes 1, 2, 3	USG	—	—	B
The Best Picture Cookbook Yet	PEK	—	—	W/B
The Calendar	FJA	MS	—	SW
The Calendar	CDL	GR2–8	—	SW
The Healthy Heart Cookbook	USG	—	—	B
The Public Health Consequences of Disasters, 1989	USG	—	—	B
The Time Is Now	PRO	EL–AD	1.0	W
Time & Money	CUI	GR3–6	—	B/W
Time & Telling Time	FJA	EL–JH	2.9	W
Tune Up & Maintenance, Parts I & II	LLS	—	—	V
U.S. Postal Service 1990 National Five-Digit ZIP Code & Post Office Directory	USG	—	—	RB
Understanding Contracts	ESW	—	—	SW
Using Dollars & Sense	FJA	—	—	W
Using Phone Books	FJA	JH–HS	2.0–3.5	W
Using a Telephone	PRO	MS–AD	—	K
Using the Newspaper to Teach Basic Living Skills	FJA	HS	—	DM
Using the Newspaper to Teach Basic Living Skills	EBS	HS	3.0	DM
Using Want Ads	FJA	JH–HS	2.0–3.5	W
Wood-Frame House Construction	USG	—	—	B
Word Works: Survival Words—Health Education	EBS	JH–SH	—	SW
Writing for Life	GLO	—	—	W

HOME MANAGEMENT *(continued)*

Material	Publisher	Age Level	Reading Level	Type
Writing Friendly Letters, Business Letters, & Resumes	FJA	HS	—	A/W
Young Homemakers Cookbook	FJA	—	—	B

FINANCIAL MANAGEMENT

Material	Publisher	Age Level	Reading Level	Type
A Course in Coins	MEM	MS–HS		W
Advertising: How It Affects You	ESW	—	—	SW
Amusement Park	SRA	—	—	G
Applied Mathematics	MEM	NS	—	W
Automobiles	MEM	—	—	W
Bank Account	FJA	MS–JH	—	G
Banking Practice Kit	LCM	—	—	K
Banking Stamps	FJA	MS–HS	—	ST
Basic Sewing	FJA	JH–HS	2.0–3.5	W
Be Credit Wise	FJA	JH–HS	2.5	W
Being with Housemates, Part 1 & 2	JMS	—	—	V
Bonds	LLS	—	—	V
Budgeting	FJA	JH–HS	2.2–2.6	W
Budgeting & Spending Skills—1	FJA	JH–HS	2.2–2.6	W
Budgeting & Spending Skills—2	FJA	JH–HS	2.2–2.6	W
Buyer Beware	ESW	—	—	SW
Buying & Caring for Clothes	FJA	JH–HS	2.0–3.5	W
Buying a Home	MEM	—	—	W
Buying with Sense	FJA	—	—	W
Calculator Activities	FJA	HS	—	DM
Career Math Makes Sense	FJA	—	—	W
Caring for Your Car	FJA	JH–HS	2.5–4.0	W
Check Writing Program	EDM	—	—	K
Checking Account	FJA	JH–HS	2.2–2.5	W
Classroom Cash	EDM	—	—	K
Coin Stamps	SRA	—	—	ST
Coins and Bills	SRA	—	—	G
Coins Skills Curriculum, Revised	EDM	EL	—	TR
Comparison Shopping	MEM	—	—	W
Complete Real-Life Math Video Series	EDI	—	—	V/W
Concerning Consumers	EDI	—	—	V/FS
Consumer Contracts	MEM	—	—	W
Consumer Math	EAC	—	—	K
Consumer Math	LCM	—	3.5–4.5	DM
Consumer Matter	EAC	—	—	K
Consumer Rights	MEM	—	—	W
Consumer Skills	FJA	HS	—	DM
Consumer Skills Poster Pak	LCM	—	3.0–3.5	P/DM
Coping with Conversions	LCM	—	4.0–5.0	DM
Counting Money & Making Change	EBS	MS–HS	2.0	DM

FINANCIAL MANAGEMENT *(continued)*

Material	Publisher	Age Level	Reading Level	Type
Credit	MEM	—	—	W
Credit Ability Game	LCM	—	4.0–5.5	G
Credit: The First Steps	ESW	—	—	SW
Crosscountry U.S.A.	ERE	—	—	SW
Deals on Wheels	FJA	HS	3.0–4.0	W
Department Store Math	FJA	MS–JH	—	G
Directory for Federal Aid	LLS	—	—	B
Dollar Daze	MEM	MS–AD	2.5	W
English for Everyday Living	FJA	MS–HS	—	DM
Everyday Consumer English	LCM	—	4.5–6.0	B
Everyday Living & Related Math	FJA	JH–HS	—	K
Everything You Need to Know About Financial Aid	LLS	—	—	V
Exploring Measurement, Time, and Money	EDM	EL	—	SW
Filling Out Forms	FJA	HS	—	A/W
Finding a Good Used Car	FJA	JH–HS	2.0–3.5	W
Forms	FJA	JH–HS	2.2–2.6	W
Forms in Your Future	GLO	—	—	W
Handling Money	EDI	MS–AD	—	V/FS
How to Buy a Home with Nothing Down	LLS	—	—	V
How to Buy a Used Car	LCM	—	—	V
How to Finance a College Education	LLS	—	—	V
How to Make the Right College Choice	LLS	—	—	V
How to Manage Your Money	SRA	MS–HS	2.5–5.0	W
How to Use Bank Accounts	SRA	MS–HS	2.5–5.0	W
How to Use the Classified Ads	SRA	MS–HS	2.5–5.0	W
How To Write 2: Forms and More	ENT	—	—	W
In a Family Way	FJA	HS	3.0–4.0	W
In Search Of Services	PEK	—	—	G
Indoor Signs	MEM	MS–AD	2.4	W
Insurance	MEM	—	—	W
Insurance: Sorting It All Out	ESW	—	—	SW
Insure Yourself	FJA	JH–HS	2.5	W
Job Applications & Other Forms	MEM	HS–AD	2.0–4.0	W
Know Your Government	LLS	—	—	B
Know Your Rights	FJA	JH–HS	2.5	W
Labels	MEM	—	—	W
Layoff	FJA	HS	3.0–4.0	W
Let's Calculate Activities	LCM	—	3.0–4.0	DM
Life Skills English	MEM	MS–AD	2.8	B/W
Life Skills Listening	EDI	MS–AD	2.0–4.0	A/W

FINANCIAL MANAGEMENT (continued)

Material	Publisher	Age Level	Reading Level	Type
Life Skills Mathematics	MEM	MS–AD	—	K
Life Skills Reading Book 1	EDI	—	3.0–5.0	W
Living Math	PEK	JH–AD	2.0–4.0	I/TR
Living on Your Own: An Independent Living Simulation	FJA	JH–HS	—	DM
Living Skills Series Book 1: A New Look at Yourself	EDI	MS–HS	—	W
Living Skills Series Book 3: Entering the Adult World	EDI	HS	—	W
Make Your Money Grow	FJA	JH–HS	2.5	W
Making Change	EBS	MS–SH	—	SW
Master Your Money	FJA	JH–HS	2.5	W
Math for Employment	EDI	MS–AD	3.0–4.0	W
Math for Everyday Living	EAC	—	4.0–6.0	SW
Math for Everyday Living	EAC	MS–AD	—	A/B
Math for Everyday Living	LCM	—	3.5–4.5	SW
Math for Food Service Occupations	EDI	MS–AD	3.0–4.0	W
Math for Successful Living	FJA	HS	—	SW
Math for the Consumer	MEM	HS	—	W
Math for the World of Work	EDI	MS–AD	4.0–6.0	W
Math Map Trip	EAC	EL	—	K
Math Survival: Checking Accounts	MEM	MS–HS	1.3	W
Math Survival: Checking Accounts/Checks & Stubs Problem Book	MEM	MS–HS	1.3	W
Math Survival: Checks & Stubs	MEM	MS–HS	1.3	W
Math Survival: Drills on Bills	MEM	MS–HS	1.3	W
Math Survival: Grocery Bills	MEM	MS–HS	1.3	W
Mathematics for Consumers	MEM	MS–AD	—	K
Mathematics in Daily Living	LCM	—	4.0–6.0	W
Medical Insurance & Benefits	MEM	—	—	W
Medicare Physician Payment	USG	—	—	B
Modern Consumer Education	EDI	—	—	W/A
D.A.D.D.Y. & M.O.M.M.Y	PEK	—	—	CP
Money	CDL	MS–HS	—	SW
Money Big Box	SRA	—	—	K
Money Flashcards	EDM	—	—	FC
Money Game	SRA	—	—	G
Money Handling	EDM	—	—	F/A
Money Makes Sense	FJA	—	—	W
Money Management	CDL	MS–HS	—	SW

FINANCIAL MANAGEMENT (continued)

Material	Publisher	Age Level	Reading Level	Type
Money Math	EDI	MS–AD	2.0–3.0	W
Money Matters	SRA	—	—	W
Money Matters	ESW	EL–AD	2.0	SW
Money Matters	COM	—	—	SW
Money Skills	EDM	EL	—	SW
Money Wise	SRA	—	—	K
Mr. & Ms.	FJA	HS	3.0–4.0	W
Mutual Funds	LLS	—	—	V
My Checkbook	ERE	—	—	SW
Number Power	CON	HS–AD	—	W
Number Sense	CON	HS–AD	—	W
Occupational Notebook	EDM	MS–HS	—	W
One More for the Road	FJA	HS	3.0–4.0	W
Ordering From Catalogs	PEK	—	—	W
Owning a Car	FJA	JH–HS	2.2–2.5	W
Pay by Check	FJA	JH–HS	2.5	W
Payday! Managing Your Paycheck	FJA	JH–HS	2.5–4.0	W
Paying Physicians: Choices for Medicare	USG	—	—	B
Paying With Cash	FJA	JH–HS	2.2–2.6	W
Paying With Promises	FJA	JH–HS	2.2–2.6	W
Planning for Your Own Apartment	FJA	JH–HS	3.0	W
Practice Money Skills	EDM	EL	—	B
Real Life Activities	MEM	MS–AD	2.4	K
Real-Life Math	PRO	JH–HS	4.5–6.0	K
Real Life Reading: Shops & Services	MEM	MS–AD	2.4	W
Real Numbers	CON	HS–AD	—	W
Real-Life Math Video Series	EDI	—	—	V
Renting	MEM	—	—	W
Retirement	USG	—	—	B
Saving	MEM	—	—	W
Scholarships Today	LLS	—	—	SW
Shopping Bag	FJA	GR2–8	—	G
Shopping Lists Games	SRA	—	—	G
Shopping Smart	ATT	—	—	K
Stepping Out	HIN	EL–AD	—	B/W
Simply English	MEM	—	—	W
Social Legislation & Taxes	EDI	—	—	FS
Specially Produced for Special Ed	ATT	—	—	K
Strategic Skill Builders for Banking	FJA	—	—	W
Strategies for Solving Math Word Problems	EDI	MS–AD	3.0–4.0	W

FINANCIAL MANAGEMENT *(continued)*

Material	Publisher	Age Level	Reading Level	Type
Survival Math Skills	LCM	—	4.5–5.5	W
Tax Time	FJA	HS	3.0–4.0	W
Taxes	MEM	—	—	W
The Consumer Series Set	MEM	—	—	K
The Data Bank Math Machine	CDL	All	—	SW
The Marketplace	LLS	—	—	V
The Wallet War	SRA	MS–HS	4.0–5.0	W
Understanding Contracts	ESW	—	—	SW
Understanding the Business World and Stocks	LLS	—	—	V
Using a Calculator	EBS	—	—	DM
Using Dollars & Sense	FJA	—	—	W
Using the Newspaper to Teach Basic Living Skills	EBS	HS	3.0	DM
Word Works: Survival Words—Health Education	EBS	JH–HS	—	SW
Working Makes Sense	LCM	—	3.5–4.5	W
Writing Checks	MEM	MS–AD	3.0	W
Writing for Life	GLO	—	—	W
You & Your Money	EDI	JH–AD	3.0–6.0	W
Your Checking Account	EBS	HS	3.0	W
Your Checking Account: Lessons in Personal Banking	FJA	HS	—	DM

FAMILY LIFE

Material	Publisher	Age Level	Reading Level	Type
Babysitting Basics	ESW	MS–AD	3.0–4.0	SW
Basic Health: Wellness & Lifestyle	MEM	NS	—	K
Being a Smarter Consumer	HEL	JH	—	F
Buying & Caring for Clothes	FJA	JH–HS	2.0–3.5	W
Cooking Class	PCI	—	—	G
Eating Right	FJA	JH–HS	3.5–4.0	W
Family Living & Sex Education	GLO	—	—	W
Family Relationships	MEM	—	—	W
Family: A Cross-Cultural Study	EDI	—	—	V/FS
Food Chains	ESW	EL	—	SW
Food Labels	ESW	—	—	SW
Forecasting the Weather	ESW	EL	—	SW
Getting Ready to Cook	FJA	—	—	W
Grounded for Life	EBS	—	—	V/B
Healthy Meal Planning	ESW	—	—	V
Healthy Meal Planning Away from Home	ESW	—	—	V
In a Family Way	FJA	HS	3.0–4.0	W
Life Cycles	ESW	EL	4.0	SW
Life Horizons II	JMS	—	—	S
Living Skills Series Book 1: A New Look at Yourself	EDI	MS–HS	—	W
Measuring for Cooking	FJA	JH–HS	2.0–3.5	W
Money Matters	HEL	—	3.0	SW
Planning Healthy Meals	FJA	JH–HS	2.0–3.5	W
Planning Meals & Shopping	FJA	—	—	W
Positive Parenting	ESW	—	—	SW
PREP for Effective Family Living	AGS	HS	—	K
Reading & Following Recipes	FJA	JH–HS	2.0–3.5	W
Responsibilities of Parenthood	MEM	—	—	W
Sharing an Apartment	FJA	JH–HS	2.5–4.0	W
Teenage Parents	LLS	HS	—	V
Writing for Life	GLO	—	—	W
Young Homemakers Cookbook	FJA	—	—	B

CHILD REARING

Material	Publisher	Age Level	Reading Level	Type
Baby-Sitting: The Responsible Way	LRS	MS–HS	—	V
Babysitting Basics	ESW	MS–AD	3.0–4.0	SW
Books for Children: No. 5, 1989	USG	—	—	B
Child Health Care	MEM	—	—	W
Deals on Wheels	FJA	HS	3.0–4.0	W
Employers & Child Care	USG	—	—	B
Family Relationships	MEM	—	—	W
First Aid & Home Safety	FJA	MS–HS	3.5–5.0	W
HELP—First Steps to First Aid	FJA	MS–HS	2.3–3.0	W
HELP—First Aid & Biology	FJA	MS–HS	2.3–3.0	W
Home & School Cooperation	MEM	—	—	W
How to Help Your Children Achieve in School	USG	—	—	B
Infant Care	USG	—	—	B
Introduction to Computers for Children	LLS	—	—	V
Learn to Use Money Wisely for Children	LLS	—	—	V
Medical Care	FJA	MS–HS	3.5–5.0	W
Plans for Living	FJA	MS–HS	2.3–3.0	W
Positive Parenting	ESW	—	—	SW
Reading Realities	ERE	EL–HS	2.0–6.0	SW
Responsibilities of Parenthood	MEM	—	—	W
Science Discovery for Children	LLS	—	—	V
Staying Healthy	FJA	MS–HS	3.5–5.0	W
Stories for Parents	CON	HS–AD	1.0–3.0	W/B
Taking Care of Yourself	FJA	MS–HS	2.3–3.0	W
Teen Problems	EDI	—	—	V
Teenage Parents	LLS	HS	—	V
The Art of Creating Crafts for Children	LLS	—	—	V
The Art of Making Pictures for Children	LLS	—	—	V
What Do You Really Want for Your Children?	LLS	—	—	V
When Baby Comes Home	HEL	JH–AD	2.5	B
Your Child from One to Six	USG	—	—	B

INDOOR ACTIVITIES

Material	Publisher	Age Level	Reading Level	Type
An Illustrated Guide to Electrical Safety	USG	—	—	B
Basic Electricity	USG	—	—	B
Fifty Birds of Town & City	USG	—	—	B
Foundation of Library Skills Series	ERE	—	—	SW
I Can	PRO	—	—	TR
Knitting, Crochet, Quilting: Advanced Methods	LRS	—	—	V
Knitting, Crochet, Quilting: The Basics	LRS	—	—	V
Life Skills Mathematics	MEM	MS–AD	—	K
Math Football Package	CDL	MS–HS	—	SW
Newspaper Literacy	EAC	—	—	SW/CP
Real Reading	EBS	GR4–HS	—	I
Real Reference	EBS	—	—	I
Stars in Your Eyes: A Guide to the Northern Skies	USG	—	—	B
Your Pet, Your Pal	LLS	—	—	V

OUTDOOR ACTIVITIES

Material	Publisher	Age Level	Reading Level	Type
I Can	PRO	—	—	TR
Plant Propagation Kit	CUI	GR5–9	—	K
Safe Living Reading Series	EAC	HS	2.5	K
Stars in Your Eyes: A Guide to the Northern Skies	USG	—	—	B
Walking for Exercise & Pleasure	USG	—	—	B

COMMUNITY/NEIGHBORHOOD ACTIVITIES

Material	Publisher	Age Level	Reading Level	Type
A Night on the Town	SRA	MS–HS	4.0–5.0	W
Dining Out	ESW	—	—	SW
Using Phone Books	FJA	JH–HS	2.0–3.5	W

TRAVEL

Material	Publisher	Age Level	Reading Level	Type
Around the World in However Many Days It Takes	LCM	—	4.0–5.0	DM
Crash	PEK	—	—	G
Crosscountry U.S.A.	ERE	—	—	SW
Everglades Wildguide: The Natural History of Everglades National Park, Florida	USG	—	—	B
Exploring Your World: States Race	MEM	NS	—	G
Exploring Your World: City Limits	MEM	NS	—	G
Finding Your Way	FJA	EL–JH	2.6	W
Government in Action	SAD	MS–AD	2.5–4.0	B/DM
In the Driver's Seat	PEK	—	3.0	K
Learning About Geography, Maps, & Globes	EAC	—	—	SW
Map Skills	ERE	—	—	SW
Math for Everyday Living	SAD	JH–HS	4.5–5.0	B
Mathematics for Consumers	MEM	MS–AD	—	K
Outdoor Signs	MEM	MS–AD	2.4	W
Railroad Maps of North America: The First Hundred Years	USG	—	—	B
Reading Schedules	FJA	JH–HS	2.0–3.5	W
Real Life Reading: Travel	MEM	MS–AD	2.4	W
So You Thought You Couldn't Read a Map	LCM	—	4.0–5.0	DM
Space Commander: A States & Capitals Game	FJA	GR3–12	—	SW
States & Capitals	FJA	MS–HS	—	SW
Survival Math	SAD	JH–AD	2.0–4.0	DM/A
Survival Vocabulary	EBS	—	—	DM
Taking a Trip	FJA	EL–HS	3.2	W
The Statue of Liberty Exhibit	USG	—	—	P
U.S. Map Games	SRA	EL	—	G
Using Maps: Concepts & Skills	FJA	—	—	DM
Using Phones and Phonebooks	PEK	—	—	W
Washington, D.C.: Official National Park Guidebook	USG	—	—	B
Where I Am	SRA	—	—	W
Writing Notes and Letters	PEK	—	—	B
Yosemite	USG	—	—	B

ENTERTAINMENT

Material	Publisher	Age Level	Reading Level	Type
A Night on the Town	SRA	MS–HS	4.0–5.0	W
Dining Out	ESW	—	—	SW
How to Use the Newspaper	SRA	MS–HS	2.5–5.0	W
Menu Math	LCM	—	3.0–4.0	DM
On My Own With Language	LSI	MS–HS	4.5–5.5	DM
Reading a Newspaper	FJA	JH–HS	2.0–3.5	W
Real Life Reading: Television	MEM	MS–AD	2.4	W
Restaurant Rookie	PEK	—	—	DM
Safe Living Reading Series	EAC	HS	2.5	K
Stepping Out	ATT	—	—	K
Survival Vocabularies: Entertainment Language	FJA	JH–HS	3.0	W

CITIZENSHIP

Material	Publisher	Age Level	Reading Level	Type
20th Century America	STV	AD	6.0–7.0	W
A Good Citizen at Home	MEM	MS–AD	2.0–4.0	W
America's Early Years	STV	AD	6.0–7.0	W
American Government	FJA	MS–HS	—	TP
American Government and Its Citizens	ENT	—	—	W
American Government: How It Works	ENT	—	—	W
Becoming An Informed Citizen	STV	AD	6.0	W
Being with Authority Figures	JMS	—	—	V
By the People . . . U.S. Government Structure	USG	—	—	B
Citizens Today	STV	AD	6.0–7.0	W
Citizenship	EAC	—	5.0	B
Citizenship & the Law	JMS	—	—	S/V/FS
Constitutional Rights	MEM	—	—	W
Consumers & the Law	EAC	—	—	SW
Crash	PEK	—	—	G
Creating the U.S. Constitution	EAC	—	—	SW
Democracy in Action	LCM	—	6.0–7.0	W/B
Election Special	ENT	—	—	B
Forms in Your Future	GLO	—	—	W
Government and Civics Series	SAD	MS–AD	2.5	B/W
Government at Work	FJA	JH–HS	2.5–5.0	W
How the Law Works	LCM	—	4.5–5.5	DM
How To Write 2: Forms and More	ENT	—	—	W
How We Got the Vote	LLS	—	—	V
In the Driver's Seat	PEK	—	3.0	K
In Your Community	FJA	EL–JH	2.7–3.1	W
In Your Country	FJA	EL–JH	2.7–3.1	W
In Your State	FJA	EL–JH	2.7–3.1	W
Juveniles Have Rights, Too	FJA	JH–HS	7.0–7.9	W
Keys to Responsible Driving	LCM	—	4.0–5.0	SW
Know Your Government	LLS	—	—	B
Know Your Rights	FJA	EL–JH	2.7–3.1	W
Learning About Government	MEM	MS–HS	—	W
Legal Services	MEM	—	—	W
Living In the U.S.A.	SAD	JH–AD	—	B/W
Living Skills Series Book 2: New Rights & Responsibilities	EDI	HS	—	W
Living Skills Series Book 3: Entering the Adult World	EDI	HS	—	W
Look at the U.S.	CON	HS–AD	—	B/W

CITIZENSHIP (continued)

Material	Publisher	Age Level	Reading Level	Type
Math for Everyday Living	SAD	JH–HS	4.5–5.0	B
Modern Consumer Education	EDI	—	—	W/A
My Country—The U.S.A.	STV	AD	2.0–3.0	W
Our American Constitution	STV	JH–HS	7.0–8.0	W
Our Constitution: The Document That Gave Birth to a Nation	ENT	—	—	V
Our Democracy	STV	JH–HS	7.0–8.0	W
Our Government in Action	FJA	JH–HS	2.5–5.0	W
Participating in Government	FJA	MS–HS	2.5	W
Respect for the Law	MEM	—	—	W
Responsibilities of Citizenship	MEM	—	—	W
Social Legislation & Taxes	MEM	—	—	W
State & Local Government	FJA	MS–HS	2.5	W
Studying for a Driver's License	LCM	—	3.5–4.5	W
Survival Math	SAD	JH–AD	2.0–4.0	DM/A
Survival Signs	HEL	—	—	SW
Teacher's Guide to the Constitution	HIN	—	—	TR
The Citizen Series Set	MEM	—	—	W
The Constitution & the Government of the U.S.	EAC	—	—	SW
The Constitution of the United States of America	USG	—	—	B
The Judicial System	MEM	—	—	W
The Roots of the Bill of Rights	LLS	—	—	B
The United States Government Manual 1989/1990	USG	—	—	B
U.S. Government in Action Resource Program	MEM	—	—	K
U.S. Government Series	HIN	—	—	B
Understanding Law	EAC	—	—	V/F
United States Citizenship	MEM	MS–HS	—	W
United States Constitution	PEK	—	3.0	W
United States Government	MEM	—	—	W
Voting	MEM	—	—	W
Washington, D.C.: Official National Park Guidebook	USG	—	—	B
We the People of the United States	ENT	—	—	W
You & the Law	MEM	MS–HS	—	W
You Are the Driver	LCM	—	4.0–5.0	W
You Are the Judge	LCM	—	5.0–6.0	W
You Are the Mayor	ENT	—	—	W
You Can Change the Law	FJA	JH–HS	7.0–7.9	W
Your Government	FJA	JH–HS	4.0	W
Your State and Its Constitution	PEK	—	—	W
Your Rights & the Law	FJA	JH–HS	4.0	W

COMMUNITY AWARENESS

Material	Publisher	Age Level	Reading Level	Type
American Holidays	LCM	—	3.7–4.5	B
Around the World in However Many Days it Takes	LCM	—	4.0–5.0	DM
Auto Safety	MEM	—	—	W
Becoming a Driver	FJA	JH–HS	2.0–3.5	W
Community Signs	COM	—	—	SW
Community Skills	PCI	—	—	G
Developing Functional Reading Skills	MEM	MS–HS	4.0–6.0	W
Dining Out	ESW	—	—	SW
Employment Signs	ATT	—	—	SW
Enjoying the Newspaper	EDI	MS–AD	—	W
Exploring Your World: States Race	MEM	NS	—	G
Exploring Your World: City Limits	MEM	NS	—	G
Finding A Good Used Car	FJA	JH–HS	2.0–3.5	W
Finding Your Way	FJA	EL–JH	2.6	W
Focus on Function	CSB	HS–AD	—	CP
Get That License	FJA	JH–HS	2.2–2.5	W
Getting Around Cities & Towns	FJA	JH–HS	2.0–3.5	W
Getting Help	FJA	JH–HS	2.5–4.0	W
Give Me a Call	FJA	MS–HS	2.8	W
Government and Civics Series	SAD	MS–AD	2.5	B/W
Government at Work	FJA	JH–HS	2.5–5.0	W
Handbook for Citizenship Kit	LCM	—	2.5–4.5	A/B
HELP! First Steps to First Aid	FJA	JH–HS	2.0–3.5	W
How to Use Maps & Directories	SRA	MS–HS	2.5–5.0	W
How to Use Schedules	SRA	MS–HS	2.5–5.0	W
In Your Community	FJA	EL–JH	2.7–3.1	W
In Your Country	FJA	EL–JH	2.7–3.1	W
In Your State	FJA	EL–JH	2.7–3.1	W
Indoor Signs	MEM	MS–AD	2.4	W
Juveniles Have Rights, Too	FJA	JH–HS	7.0–7.9	W
Know Your Rights	FJA	EL–JH	2.7–3.1	W
Learning About Geography, Maps, & Globes	EAC	—	—	SW
Life Coping Skills Series: Facts & Sources	STV	MS–JH	2.0–4.0	W
Life Coping Skills Series: Signs & Labels	STV	MS–JH	2.0–4.0	W
Life Skills Driving	EDI	HS	4.0–5.0	W
Life Skills English	MEM	MS–AD	2.8	B/W
Look at the U.S.	CON	HS–AD	—	B/W
Map Skills	ERE	—	—	SW
Map Skills	CDL	—	—	SW
Medical Words	ATT	—	—	SW

COMMUNITY AWARENESS (continued)

Material	Publisher	Age Level	Reading Level	Type
New Reports	PEK	—	—	A/W
Newspower Study Skills	SAD	MS–HS	4.5–5.5	W
Our Government in Action	FJA	JH–HS	2.5–5.0	W
Outdoor Signs	MEM	MS–AD	2.4	W
Participating in Government	FJA	MS–HS	2.5	W
Railroad Maps of North America: The First Hundred Years	USG	—	—	B
Reading & Following Directions	FJA	JH–HS	2.0–3.5	W
Reading a Newspaper	FJA	JH–HS	2.0–3.5	W
Reading for Successful Living	FJA	JH–HS	—	SW
Reading Schedules	FJA	JH–HS	2.0–3.5	W
Real Life Activities	MEM	MS–AD	2.4	K
Signs & Symbols	ESW	—	—	SW
So You Thought You Couldn't Read a Map	LCM	—	4.0–5.0	DM
Space Commander: A States & Capitals Game	FJA	GR3–12	—	SW
Survival Signs	COM	—	—	SW
Survival Skills System	CNV	—	—	SW
Survival Words	COM	—	—	SW
Taking a Trip	FJA	EL–HS	3.2	W
The Telephone Book Can Tell You	FJA	JH–HS	2.2–2.5	W
Transportation Signs	ATT	—	—	SW
U.S. Map Games	SRA	EL	—	G
Using Maps: Concepts & Skills	FJA	—	—	DM
Using Phone Books	FJA	JH–HS	2.0–3.5	W
What's Happening	PEK	—	—	W
Where I Am	SRA	—	—	G
Winterberry City	CSB	HS–AD	—	G
You Tell Me	PCI	—	—	G
You Can Change the Law	FJA	JH–HS	7.0–7.9	W
Your Government	FJA	JH–HS	4.0	W
Your Rights and the Law	FJA	JH–HS	4.0	W

SERVICES/RESOURCES

Material	Publisher	Age Level	Reading Level	Type
Auto Safety	MEM	—	—	W
Becoming a Driver	FJA	JH–HS	2.0–3.5	W
Caring	FJA	HS	3.0–4.0	W
Directory for Federal Aid	LLS	—	—	B
Emergency	FJA	HS	3.0–4.0	W
Finding Your Way	FJA	EL–JH	2.6	W
Getting Help	FJA	JH–HS	2.5–4.0	W
HELP! First Steps to First Aid	FJA	JH–HS	2.0–3.5	W
How the Law Works	LCM	—	4.5–5.5	DM
Know Your Government	LLS	—	—	B
Layoff	FJA	HS	3.0–4.0	W
Life Coping Skills Series: Facts & Sources	STV	MS–JH	2.0–4.0	W
Life Skills Driving	EDI	HS	4.0–5.0	W
Life Skills English	MEM	MS–AD	2.8	B/W
Living In the U.S.A.	SAD	JH–AD	—	B/W
Living Skills Series Book 2: New Rights & Responsibilities	EDI	HS	—	W
Need a Doctor	FJA	JH–HS	2.5–4.0	W
Occupational Notebook	EDM	MS–HS	—	W
Outdoor Signs	MEM	MS–AD	2.4	W
Reading Schedules	FJA	JH–HS	2.0–3.5	W
Real Life Reading: Shops & Services	MEM	MS–AD	2.4	W
Real Life Reading: Telephone	MEM	MS–AD	2.4	W
U.S. Map Games	SRA	EL	—	G
Using the Newspaper to Teach Basic Living Skills	FJA	HS	—	DM
Where I Am	SRA	—	—	G
Winterberry City	CSB	HS–AD	—	G
You & the Law	MEM	MS–HS	—	W

PHYSICAL HEALTH

Material	Publisher	Age Level	Reading Level	Type
800 Cocaine	LCM	—	5.5–7.0	B
A Kid's Guide Video Series	EDM	EL	—	V
ABO Blood Simutype Kit	CUI	GR5–12	—	K
AIDS Update	GLO	—	—	W
AIDS: What We Need to Know	PRO	JH–HS	—	TRW
AIDS: What You Don't Know Can Kill You	LCM	—	5.0–5.5	B
Alcohol & Tobacco	GLO	—	—	W
Alcohol & You	EDM	MS–JH	—	V
Answers About AIDS	PEK	—	—	W
Are You Healthy and Safe	PEK	—	—	K
Back on the Street	LCM	—	—	V
Basic Health: Wellness & Lifestyle	MEM	NS	—	K
Beginning Health & Nutrition	CUI	GR3–7	—	K
Blood & Guts	CUI	GR3–9	—	B
Bodywatch	LLS	—	—	V
Breaking Bad Habits: Techniques that Work	EBS	MS–HS	4.0	P
Changing Inappropriate Sexual Behavior	EDM	—	—	TR
Child Health Care	MEM	—	—	W
Circles I: Intimacy & Relationships	JMS	—	—	S
Circles III: Safer Ways	JMS	—	—	S/V
Cleaning Up Your Act	SRA	MS–HS	4.0–5 0	W
Cocaine and Crack	LCM	—	—	V
Crack	EAC	—	—	V/F
Dietary Guidelines for Americans	USG	—	—	B
Drug Alert	SAD	MS–HS	—	SW
Drug Alert	ERE	MS–HS	—	SW
Drugs & You	EDM	MS–JH	—	V
Drugs, Cigarettes, & Alcohol	MEM	—	—	W
Drugs: Uses & Abuses	GLO	—	—	W
Eating Better When Eating Out: Using the Dietary Guidelines	USG	—	—	B
Eating Right	FJA	JH–HS	3.5–4.0	W
Emergency	FJA	HS	3.0–4.0	W
Encyclopedia of Good Health	LCM	—	5.0–7.0	B
Family Living & Sex Education	GLO	—	—	W
First Aid	MEM	—	—	W
First Aid & Home Safety	FJA	MS–HS	3.5–5.0	W
First Aid Book	USG	—	—	B
Food and Nutrition	HEL	HS	2.0	TR
Food for Thought	SUN	MS–AD	—	SW

PHYSICAL HEALTH *(continued)*

Material	Publisher	Age Level	Reading Level	Type
Good Grooming Habits	EPR	JH–AD	<4.0	WB
Guidelines for Protecting the Safety & Health of Health Care Workers	USG	—	—	B
Health United States, 1988	USG	—	—	B
Health Video & Films	EAC	—	—	V/F
HELP! First Steps to First Aid	FJA	JH–HS	2.0–3.5	W
HELP: First Aid and Biology	FJA	MS–HS	2.3–3.0	W
High Interest Health	LCM	—	6.0–7.5	B
Human Senses Classroom Kit	CUI	GR5–12	—	K
Human Sexuality	EDM	—	—	TR
In a Family Way	FJA	HS	3.0–4.0	W
Infant Care	USG	—	—	B
It's There, But You Can't See It	LCM	—	4.0–5.0	DM
Keeping Fit	FJA	JH–HS	3.5–4.0	W
Kitchen Safety	HEL	HS–AD	—	V
Know Your Body	PEK	—	—	W
Learning First Aid	MEM	MS–AD	—	W
Life Horizons I	JMS	—	—	S
Life Horizons II	JMS	—	—	S
Life Science Activities	CUI	GR2–8	—	TR
LifeFacts 1	JMS	—	—	K
LifeFacts 2	JMS	—	—	K
LifeFacts 3	JMS	—	—	K
Living Skills Series Book 1: A New Look at Yourself	EDI	MS–HS	—	W
Looking Good	FJA	JH–HS	3.5–4.0	W
Looking Good Key	PCI	—	—	G
Looking Good: A Guide to Personal Grooming	HEL	HS	—	V
Making Bag Lunches, Snacks, & Desserts Using the Dietary Guidelines	USG	—	—	B
Medical Care	FJA	MS–HS	3.5–5.0	W
Medicare Physician Payment	USG	—	—	B
Mini Encyclopedia on Drugs and Alcohol	LCM	—	6.5–7.5	B
National Directory of Drug Abuse and Alcoholism Treatment and Prevention Programs	USG	—	—	B
Need a Doctor	FJA	JH–HS	2.5–4.0	W
One More for the Road	FJA	HS	3.0–4.0	W
Personal Care Skills	PRO	—	—	K
Personal Health & Conduct	FJA	HS	—	FS/A
Planning Healthy Meals	FJA	JH–HS	2.0–3.5	W
Planning Meals & Shopping	FJA	—	—	W

PHYSICAL HEALTH *(continued)*

Material	Publisher	Age Level	Reading Level	Type
Plans for Living	FJA	MS–HS	2.3–3.0	W
Preparing Foods & Planning Menus Using the Dietary Guidelines	USG	—	—	B
Profile Your Lifestyle	EAC	—	—	V
Reading for Successful Living	FJA	JH–HS	—	SW
Reading Realities	ERE	EL or HS	2.0–6.0	SW
Real Facts: The Truth About Drugs	MEM	MS–AD	—	W
Real Life Reading: Medicine	MEM	MS–AD	2.4	W
Reducing the Health Consequences of Smoking: 25 Years of Progress	USG	—	—	B
Say No to Drugs	LLS	—	—	V
Self Defense for Women	LLS	—	—	V
Sex, Drugs, and AIDS	LCM	—	3.0–3.5	B
Sexuality Education for Persons with Severe Developmental Disabilities	JMS	—	—	S
Shopping for Food & Making Meals in Minutes Using the Dietary Guidelines	USG	—	—	B
Simple Cooking	EDM	—	—	B
Smoking & You	EDM	MS–JH	—	V
Smoking Experiment	CUI	GR3–12	—	K
Smokeless Tobacco Use in the United States	USG	—	—	B
Speaking of Sex	JMS	—	—	V/B/TR
Staying Healthy	FJA	MS–HS	3.5–5.0	W
Story Starters: Science	ERE	—	—	SW
Substance Abuse	LCM	—	4.0–5.0	P
Survival Vocabulary	EBS	—	—	DM
Survival Vocabulary	FJA	MS–HS	—	DM
Surviving Adolescence	LCM	—	5.5–7.0	B
Taking Care of Simple Injuries	PRO	—	—	K
Taking Care of Yourself	FJA	MS–HS	2.3–3.0	W
Teens Talk About Alcohol	LCM	—	5.0–6.0	B
The Body Transparent	ERE	MS–HS	—	SW
The Breast Center Video	LLS	—	—	V
The Facts About Drugs and Alcohol	LCM	—	5.0–6.0	B
The Healthy Heart Cookbook	USG	—	—	B
The Human Body	LCM	—	4.0–5.5	W/B
The Truth About Drugs	LCM	—	4.5–5.5	W
Understanding AIDS	EDI	MS–HS	—	W
Walking for Exercise & Pleasure	USG	—	—	B
What's Happening to My Body	LCM	—	5.0–6.0	B

PHYSICAL HEALTH *(continued)*

Material	Publisher	Age Level	Reading Level	Type
When Cocaine Affects Someone You Love	USG	—	—	B
Word Works: Survival Words—Health Education	EBS	JH–SH	—	SW
Wow! What a Mind and Body	LCM	—	4.5–5.5	DM
Your Child from One to Six	USG	—	—	B

EMOTIONAL HEALTH

Material	Publisher	Age Level	Reading Level	Type
A Kid's Guide Video Series	EDM	EL	—	V
All About You	PCI	—	—	G
Behavior Skills	PCI	—	—	G
Breaking Bad Habits: Techniques that Work	EBS	MS–HS	4.0	P
Building Self-Esteem in the Classroom: The Experts Speak	LLS	—	—	A/TR
Circles I: Intimacy & Relationships	JMS	—	—	S
Circles II: Stop Abuse	JMS	—	—	S/FS/V
Coping With Books	AGS	JH–HS	—	K
Dilemma	EAC	—	2.5	SW
Encyclopedia of Good Health	LCM	—	5.0–7.0	B
Feeling Good	FJA	JH–HS	3.5–4.0	W
Grounded for Life	EBS	—	—	V/B
Guest Advice Columnist	PEK	—	—	CP
High Interest Health	LCM	—	6.0–7.5	B
How to Say No	EBS	MS–HS	—	K
Infant Care	USG	—	—	B
Life Horizons I	JMS	—	—	S
LifeFacts 1	JMS	—	—	K
LifeFacts 2	JMS	—	—	K
Making Lemonade	PEK	—	—	CP
National Directory of Drug Abuse and Alcoholism Treatment and Prevention Programs	USG	—	—	B
Now You're Talking	EAC	—	—	K
One More for the Road	FJA	HS	3.0–4.0	W
People Working Today	EDM	MS–HS	2.0	B
Personal Power	PRO	MS–HS	—	TR
Phoenix Self Esteem Video Lab	LCM	—	5.0–6.5	V/DM
Plans for Living	FJA	MS–HS	2.3–3.0	W
Pouvant I	PRO	MS–HS	—	TR/B
Prepare Curriculum	REP	JH–HS	—	TR
Real Friends	LCM	—	5.5–6.0	B
Refusal Skill Video	REP	JH–HS	—	B/V
Refusal Skills	REP	JH–HS	—	TR
Report of the Secretary's Task Force on Youth Suicide	USG	—	—	B
Seeds of Self-Esteem	AGS	EL–JH	—	K
Self-Esteem	GLO	—	—	W
Self-Esteem in the Classroom: A Curriculum Guide	LLS	—	—	TR/B
Self-Esteem: Choice Not Chance	FJA	HS	—	V

EMOTIONAL HEALTH *(continued)*

Material	Publisher	Age Level	Reading Level	Type
Sexuality Education for Persons with Severe Developmental Disabilities	JMS	—	—	S
Skills for Living	REP	—	—	B
Smokeless Tobacco Use in the United States	USG	—	—	B
Social Skill Strategies	THK	MS–HS	6.0–7.0	B/DM
Social Skills for Daily Living	AGS	JH–HS	—	B
Stress & the Young Adult	ESW	—	5.0–6.0	SW
Surviving Adolescence	LCM	—	5.5–7.0	B
Take Charge of Your Life	LCM	—	4.0–4.5	W
TAWK	PEK	—	—	G
Teen Problems	EDI	—	—	V
Teenage Stress	LLS	MS–HS	—	V
The Dynamics of Relationships	EBS	MS–HS	—	B
When Cocaine Affects Someone You Love	USG	—	—	B
Why Can't Anyone Hear Me	LCM	—	5.5–7.5	W
You Tell Me	PCI	—	—	G
Your Child from One to Six	USG	—	—	B

PERSONAL CONFIDENCE/UNDERSTANDING

Material	Publisher	Age Level	Reading Level	Type
A Night on the Town	SRA	MS–HS	4.0–5.0	W
All About You	PCI	—	—	G
Are You Satisfied?	EDI	—	—	V
Asset: Social Skills Program for Adolescents	REP	JH–HS	—	K
Attitudes & Habits in Everyday Living	EDI	MS–AD	—	V/FS
Be a Winner: Be Assertive	ESW	—	—	SW
Be a Winner: Be Motivated	ESW	—	—	SW
Be a Winner: Set Your Goals	ESW	—	—	SW
Be a Winner: Negotiate	ESW	—	—	SW
Behavior Skills	PCI	—	—	G
Being with a Date, Parts 1 & 2	JMS	—	—	V
Being with Acquaintances & Strangers	JMS	—	—	V
Being with Authority Figures	JMS	—	—	V
Being with Friends, Parts 1 & 2	JMS	—	—	V
Big Hassle	FJA	JH–HS	2.5–4.0	W
Blueprint for Decision Making	ESW	JH–AD	3.0–4.5	SW
Building Self-Esteem in the Classroom: The Experts Speak	LLS	—	—	A/TR
Communication Skills	COM	MS–AD	4.0–5.0	SW
Ethics & You	ESW	EL	5.0–6.0	SW
Feeling Good	FJA	JH–HS	3.5–4.0	W
Getting Along with Others	EDM	EL	—	K
Give Me a Call	FJA	MS–HS	2.8	W
Go For It	LCM	—	5.0–6.0	B
Guidance & Counseling Software	CNV	—	—	SW
How to Follow Directions	SRA	MS–HS	2.5–5.0	W
How to Write Letters & Messages	SRA	MS–HS	2.4–4.0	W
Improving Your Self Concept	ESW	JH–AD	3.0–4.0	SW
Job Search Education	EDI	—	—	W
Jury Series	ENT	—	—	SW
Last Goodbye	FJA	JH–HS	2.5–4.0	W
Let's Have a Talk	FJA	MS–HS	2.8	W
Living Skills Series Book 3: Entering the Adult World	EDI	HS	—	W
Looking Good	FJA	JH–HS	3.5–4.0	W
Looking Good: A Guide to Personal Grooming	HEL	HS	—	V
Marathon	JMS	—	—	K
Me & Jobs	EDI	—	3.0–6.0	W
Me & My Future	EDI	MS–HS	5.0–8.0	W
Me & Others	EDI	MS–HS	0–6.0	W

PERSONAL CONFIDENCE/UNDERSTANDING *(continued)*

Material	Publisher	Age Level	Reading Level	Type
Mind Your Manners—Self-Confidence	JMS	—	—	V
Mind Your Manners—Social Success	JMS	—	—	V
National Directory of Drug Abuse and Alcoholism Treatment and Prevention Programs	USG	—	—	B
Oral Communication	FJA	HS	—	FS/A
Phoenix Self-Esteem Video Lab	LCM	—	5.0–6.5	V/DM
Pouvant I	PRO	MS–HS	—	TR/B
Practical Strategies for Problem Solving	LCM	—	5.0–5.5	DM
Present Yourself for Success	ESW	—	—	SW
Put Down Pro	FJA	JH–HS	2.5–4.0	W
Reading & Following Directions	FJA	JH–HS	2.0–3.5	W
Ready, Set, Study	CON	HS–AD	4.0–8.0	W
Real Friends	LCM	—	5.5–6.0	B
Real Reading	EBS	GR4–SH	—	I
Real-Life Dilemmas	ENT	—	—	SW
Report of the Secretary's Task Force on Youth Suicide	USG	—	—	B
Resource of Activities for Peer Pragmatics (RAPP)	LSI	MS–HS	0–4.5	DM
Respect: The 1st "R" on Report Cards	ACT	EL–HS	—	K
Responsibility: A Curriculum for Building Self-Esteem	LCM	—	—	TR
Responsible Assertion	REP	—	—	V
Scripting: Social Communication for Adolescents	THK	MS–HS	5.0	B
Seeds of Self-Esteem	AGS	EL–JH	—	K
Self-Esteem Poster Set	LCM	—	4.0–5.0	P
Self-Advocacy for Persons with Developmental Disabilities	JMS	—	—	V
Self-Esteem	GLO	—	—	W
Self-Esteem Connection	ACT	HS	—	V
Self-Esteem in the Classroom: A Curriculum Guide	LLS	—	—	TR/B
Self-Esteem: Choice Not Chance	FJA	HS	—	V
Skills for Job Success—Do	EPR	JH–AD	4.0	W
Skills for Job Success—Notice & Think	EPR	JH–AD	4.0	W
Skillstreaming the Adolescent	REP	MS–HS	—	B
Skillstreaming Video	REP	MS–HS	—	B/V
Smokeless Tobacco Use in the United States	USG	—	—	B
Social Competence and Employability Skills Curriculum	ASP	HS	—	TR
Social Skill Strategies	THK	MS–HS	5.0	B/DM
Specially Produced for Special Ed	EDI	—	—	FS
Stepping Out	ATT	—	—	K

PERSONAL CONFIDENCE/UNDERSTANDING *(continued)*

Material	Publisher	Age Level	Reading Level	Type
Stress & the Young Adult	ESW	—	5.0–6.0	SW
Survival Words	EBS	—	—	SW
Teen Problems	EDI	—	—	V
Tele-Trainer	EBS	MS–HS	—	K
Telephone Skills	EBS	MS–HS	—	K
The Amazing Adventures of Harvey Crumbaker	LCM	—	4.0–5.0	DM
The Choice	FJA	JH–HS	2.5–4.0	W
The Dynamics of Relationships	EBS	MS–HS	—	B
The Power of Choice	CNV	—	—	V
The Promise	FJA	JH–HS	2.5–4.0	W
The Think Aloud Series: Increasing Social & Cognitive Skills	EDM	EL	—	TR
The Waksman Social Skills Curriculum	PRO	MS–HS	—	B/W
The Walker Social Skills Program	PRO	MS–HS	—	B/W
Thinking, Feeling, Behaving: An Emotional Education Curriculum	EDM	EL	1.0–6.0	TR
Time to Change	FJA	JH–HS	2.5–4.0	W
Tips	JMS	—	—	V/S
Understanding Yourself	HEL	JH–HS	—	F
Unlocking Your Potential	LLS	—	—	A/TR
Way to Work	FJA	JH–HS	2.3	W
What Could I Say?	REP	JH–HS	—	V
When Cocaine Affects Someone You Love	USG	—	—	B
Why Can't Anyone Hear Me	LCM	—	5.5–7.5	W
Write Me a Note	FJA	MS–HS	2.8	W
You & Your Attitude	EPR	JH–AD	5.0	W
You & Your New Job Series	EDI	—	—	V
You Are . . . . Series	HIN	MS–HS	4.0–5.0	B/W
You Tell Me	PCI	—	—	G

GOAL SETTING

Material	Publisher	Age Level	Reading Level	Type
A Kid's Guide Video Series	EDM	EL	—	V
A Week in the Life of . . .	ENT	—	5.0	SW
Alcohol & Tobacco	GLO	—	—	W
Analogies	SAD	MS–HS	—	W
Are You Satisfied?	EDI	—	—	V
Asset: Social Skills Program for Adolescents	REP	JH–HS	—	K
Be a Winner: Set Your Goals	ESW	—	—	SW
Big Hassle	FJA	JH–HS	2.5–4.0	W
Blueprint for Decision Making	ESW	JH–AD	3.0–4.5	SW
Choices and Challenges in Your Future	LCM	—	5.5–7.0	W/B
College Prep Course	MEM	HS–AD	9.0–12.0	W
Communicating Day By Day	HEL	JH	—	F
Crosscountry U.S.A.	ERE	—	—	SW
Daily Communication: Strategies for the Language Disordered Adolescent	THK	MS–HS	—	B/DM
Decisions at Work	HEL	HS–AD	3.0–4.0	F/W
Dilemma	EAC	—	2.5	SW
Drug Alert	ERE	MS–HS	—	SW
Drugs: Uses & Abuses	GLO	—	—	W
Following Directions	ESW	—	—	SW
Go For It	LCM	—	5.0–6.0	B
Guest Advice Columnist	PEK	—	—	I
How to Live in the World	LLS	—	—	A/TR
How to Understand & Manage Your Time	SRA	MS–HS	2.5–5.0	W
I Don't Know What to Do	HEL	JH–HS	—	V
It's Your Choice	LCM	—	5.5–6.5	W/B
Job Survival Skills	EDI	—	3.0–6.0	W
Last Goodbye	FJA	JH–HS	2.5–4.0	W
Life Situations	LCM	—	2.0–3.5	B/DM
Living Alone	COM	HS–AD	3.0–4.0	SW
Making Lemonade	PEK	—	—	I
Making the Grade	SAD	JH–HS	—	W
Mind Games: Puzzles in Logic	SAD	MS–HS	—	W
D.A.D.D.Y. & M.O.M.M.Y.	PEK	—	—	CP
Newspower Study Skills	SAD	MS–HS	4.5–5.5	W
Now What Do I Do?	HEL	—	3.0–4.0	A/W
Practical Strategies for Problem Solving	LCM	—	5.0–5.5	DM
Prepare Curriculum	REP	JH–HS	—	TR
Problem Solving for Teens	LSI	MS–HS	2.5–3.5	W
Put Down Pro	FJA	JH–HS	2.5–4.0	W

GOAL SETTING *(continued)*

Material	Publisher	Age Level	Reading Level	Type
Reading Between the Lines	SAD	HS	—	W
Reading Realities	ERE	EL or HS	2.0–6.0	SW
Real Life Reading Workshop	LCM	—	2.0–4.0	FC/DM
Reasoning Skills on the Job	CNV	HS–AD	3.5–5.0	SW
Resource of Activities for Peer Pragmatics (RAPP)	LSI	MS–HS	4.5	DM
Scripting: Social Communication for Adolescents	THK	MS–HS	5.0	B
Social Decision-Making Skills: A Curriculum Guide for Elementary Grades	ASP	MS–HS	—	TR
Study Skills Series	SAD	MS–AD	4.5–7.5	W
Take Charge of Your Life	LCM	—	4.0–4.5	W
Teaching Behavioral Self-Control to Students	PRO	—	—	TR
The Changer and the Changed	LCM	—	6.0–7.5	B
The Choice	FJA	JH–HS	2.5–4.0	W
The Decision-Making Skillbook	EBS	MS–JH	—	W
The Promise	FJA	JH–HS	2.5–4.0	W
The Think Aloud Series: Increasing Social & Cognitive Skills	EDM	EL	—	TR
The Waksman Social Skills Curriculum	PRO	MS–HS	—	B/W
Thinking, Feeling, Behaving: An Emotional Education Curriculum	EDM	EL	1.0–6.0	TR
Time to Change	FJA	JH–HS	2.5–4.0	W
Transfer Activities: Thinking Skill Vocabulary Development	THK	MS–HS	—	B/DM
Unlocking Your Potential	LLS	—	—	A/TR
Walker Social Skills Curriculum: Access Program	PRO	JH–HS	—	TR
Why Is It Always Me?	REP	JH–HS	—	V
Working for a Living	HEL	HS–AD	—	V
You Are . . . . Series	HIN	MS–HS	4.0–5.0	B/W

SELF-IMPROVEMENT

Material	Publisher	Age Level	Reading Level	Type
125 Ways to Be a Better Student	LSI	MS–HS	Intermediate	DM
Academic Survival Tips for Student Athletes	LLS	—	—	A
Active Listening Program	THK	HS–AD	—	K
Activities for Dictionary Practice	CUR	MS–JH	—	DM
All About Manners	EDM	—	—	F/A
All About You	PCI	—	—	G
Assuming Your Responsibilities	HEL	JH–HS	—	F
Basic Skills/Study Techniques Program	LLS	—	—	K
Basic Study Skills	LCM	—	3.5–5.5	W
Being with a Date, Parts 1 & 2	JMS	—	—	V
Being with Friends, Parts 1 & 2	JMS	—	—	V
Breaking Bad Habits: Techniques that Work	EBS	MS–HS	4.0	P
Building Memory Skills	ESW	—	—	SW
Career Planning: Putting Your Skills to Work	HEL	HS–AD	—	V
Classification & Organization Skills—Developmental	CUR	HS–AD	6.0	W
College Bound	ESW	HS–AD	3.0–4.0	SW
College Life	ESW	HS–AD	3.0–4.0	SW
College Prep Course	MEM	HS–AD	9.0–12.0	W
Communicate	THK	MS–HS	—	G
Communicate Expansion Cards	THK	MS–HS	—	G
Communicating Day By Day	HEL	JH	—	F
Communication Skills	COM	MS–AD	4.0–5.0	SW
Computer Assisted Writing	EAC	—	—	SW
Computer Test Preparation	LLS	HS–AD	—	SW
Core Home and School Vocabulary	PRO	—	3–11 yrs.	K
Developing Functional Reading Skills	MEM	MS–HS	4.0–6.0	W
Dictionary Skills Practice	CUR	MS–AD	4.0	W
Effective Reading	LLS	—	—	A/W
English for Everyday Living	SAD	MS–HS	4.5–5.5	B
English Survival Series	SAD	MS–AD	2.0–5.0	W
Everyday English	SAD	JH–AD	—	W
Feeling Good	FJA	JH–HS	3.5–4.0	W
First Days on the Job	ESW	HS–AD	4.0–5.0	SW
Following Directions	ESW	—	—	SW
Footsteps	PEK	—	—	K
Foundation of Library Skills Series	ERE	—	—	SW
Getting Along with Others	EDM	EL	—	K
Getting Smarter	FJA	JH–HS	4.0–6.0	W
HomeWork Coach	AGS	JH–HS	—	K
How to Improve Your Study Skills	VGM	—	—	B

SELF-IMPROVEMENT (continued)

Material	Publisher	Age Level	Reading Level	Type
How to Prepare for College	VGM	—	—	B
How to Succeed in College	LLS	—	—	V
I Dropped Out . . . . The Series	EBS	—	—	V
I Hate School Survival Guide	LCM	—	6.5–7.5	B
Improving Your Study Skills	MEM	MS–AD	—	W
Inside Strategies for the SAT	EDI	—	—	W
Keeping Fit	FJA	JH–HS	3.5–4.0	W
Learning Improvement Series	FJA	JH–HS	3.5	SW
Letter Writing Worktext	LCM	—	4.5–5.5	W/B
Life Skills Driving	EDI	HS	4.0–5.0	W
Listening & Notetaking	EAC	—	—	A/B
Living Math	PEK	JH–AD	2.0–4.0	I/TR
Look It Up	GLO	—	—	W
Look, Listen, & Touch	ESW	—	—	SW
Looking Good: A Guide to Personal Grooming	HEL	HS	—	V
Making the Grade	SAD	JH–HS	—	W
Making the Grade	HEL	—	5.0	SW
Making the Grade	LLS	—	—	SW
Mastering Writing Skills	LCM	—	5.0–6.0	W
Mind Your Manners—Self-Confidence	JMS	—	—	V
New Reports	PEK	—	—	A/W
Newspaper Workshop: Understanding Your Newspaper	GLO	—	—	W
Newspower Study Skills	SAD	MS–HS	4.5–5.5	W
Notetaking	PEK	—	—	K
Now Is the Time	ESW	HS–AD	3.0–4.0	V
Number Power	CON	HS–AD	—	W
Number Sense	CON	HS–AD	—	W
On the Job	HEL	HS	4.0	V
Pacemaker Communication Skills	HEL	—	2.0–3.0	W
Personal Care Skills	PRO	—	—	K
Personal Power	PRO	MS–HS	—	TR
Phoenix Self-Esteem Video Lab	LCM	—	5.0–6.5	V/DM
Practical Strategies for Problem Solving	LCM	—	5.0–5.5	DM
Present Yourself for Success	ESW	—	—	SW
Ready, Set, Study	CON	HS–AD	4.0–8.0	W
Real Life Writing Skills	LCM	—	4.0–5.0	W
Real Numbers	CON	HS–AD	—	W
Real Reference	EBS	—	—	I
Research Reports	CUR	MS	—	W

SELF-IMPROVEMENT *(continued)*

Material	Publisher	Age Level	Reading Level	Type
Responsibility: A Curriculum for Building Self-Esteem	LCM	—	—	TR
Responsible Assertion	REP	—	—	V
Sack-Yourman Study Skills Program	MEM	HS–AD	9.0–12.0	K
Scripting: Social Communication for Adolescents	THK	MS–HS	5.0	B
Self-Advocacy for Persons with Developmental Disabilities	JMS	—	—	V
Simply English	HIN	EL–AD	—	B/W
Skills for Living	REP	—	—	B
Skills for School Success	CUR	EL	—	W
Skills for Successful Test Taking	ESW	—	—	SW
Skillstreaming the Adolescent	REP	MS–HS	—	B
Skillstreaming Video	REP	MS–HS	—	B/V
Social Skills at Work	HEL	HS–AD	—	V
Social Skills on the Job	HEL	HS–AD	4.0	K
Story Starters: Science	ERE	NS	—	SW
Story Starters: Social Studies	ERE	NS	—	SW
Strategies for Study	SAD	JH–HS	—	W
Strategies for Study	LCM	—	5.5–7.0	W/B
Study Aids	CON	HS–AD	—	W/B
Study Skills	ENT	—	—	SW
Study Skills	FJA	JH–HS	—	TP
Study Skills	HEL	JH–HS	—	V
Study Skills	ESW	—	—	SW
Study Skills & Strategies	MEM	HS–AD	—	W
Study Skills Series	SAD	MS–AD	4.5–7.5	W
Study Skills: Strategies & Practice	CUR	HS–AD	1.0–7.0	DM
Study Smart	THK	MS–HS	—	G
Study Smart Expansion Cards	THK	MS–HS	—	G
Study to Succeed	ESW	—	—	SW
Study: A Key to Learning	FJA	JH–HS	—	A/W
Success in the Classroom	LLS	—	—	V
Survival Vocabulary	SAD	JH–AD	2.0–4.0	B/W
Teaching Behavioral Self-Control to Students	PRO	—	—	TR
Test Ready Mathematics	CUR	HS–AD	GR1.0–8.0	WB
Test Ready Practice with Cloze	CUR	HS–AD	GR3.0–6.0	WB
Test Ready Reading & Vocabulary	CUR	HS–AD	1.0–8.0	WB
Test Taking Made Easy	ENT	—	—	SW
Test Taking Made Easy	ESW	—	—	SW
Test Taking Techniques	EAC	—	—	A/B

SELF-IMPROVEMENT (continued)

Material	Publisher	Age Level	Reading Level	Type
Test-Taking Made Easy	CDL	HS	—	SW
Tests of Applied Literacy Skills	FJA	—	—	T
The Changer and the Changed	LCM	—	6.0–7.5	B
The Dropout Prevention Program	LLS	—	—	K/TR
The Outlining Kit	CUR	MS	—	K
The Test Taker's Edge	SUN	MS–AD	—	SW
The Think Aloud Series: Increasing Social & Cognitive Skills	EDM	EL	—	TR
The Video Test Preparation Review Series	LLS	HS–AD	—	V
The Walker Social Skills Program	PRO	MS–HS	—	B/W
Thirty Lessons in Note-Taking	CUR	MS	—	W
Thirty Lessons in Outlining	CUR	JH–HS	—	W
Tips	JMS	—	—	V/S
Transfer Activities: Thinking Skill Vocabulary Development	THK	MS–HS	—	B/DM
Typing	FJA	MS–HS	—	SW
United States Constitution	PEK	—	3.0	W
Unlocking Test Taking	GLO	—	—	W
Unlocking Your Potential	LLS	—	—	A/TR
Vocabulary Building	SAD	MS–HS	—	DM
Vocabulary in Context	PRO	—	1.5–6.0	TR
Walker Social Skills Curriculum: ACCEPTS Program	PRO	EL	—	B/TR
Walker Social Skills Curriculum: ACCESS Program	PRO	JH–HS	—	B/TR
What Could I Say?	REP	JH–HS	—	V
What Would You Do If You Knew You Couldn't Fail	LCM	—	—	V
What's Happening	PEK	—	—	W
Why Can't Anyone Hear Me	LCM	—	5.5–7.5	W
Why Stay in School	EBS	—	—	V/DM
Work Habits and Attitudes	HEL	HS–AD	—	F
Writing Competency Practice	EAC	HS	—	B/DM
Your State and Its Constitution	PEK	—	—	W

RELATIONSHIPS

Material	Publisher	Age Level	Reading Level	Type
AIDS: What You Don't Know Can Kill You	LCM	—	5.0–5.5	B
Are You Satisfied?	EDI	—	—	V
Attitudes & Habits in Everyday Living	EDI	MS–AD	—	V/FS
Basic Home Economics	MEM	MS–AD	—	K
Be a Winner: Negotiate	ESW	—	—	SW
Behavior Skills	PCI	—	—	G
Being with a Date, Parts 1 & 2	JMS	—	—	V
Being with Acquaintances & Strangers	JMS	—	—	V
Being with Authority Figures	JMS	—	—	V
Being with Friends, Parts 1 & 2	JMS	—	—	V
Being with Housemates, Parts 1 & 2	JMS	—	—	V
Big Hassle	FJA	JH–HS	2.5–4.0	W
Blueprint for Decision Making	ESW	JH–AD	3.0–4.5	SW
Changing Inappropriate Sexual Behavior	EDM	—	—	TR
Circles I: Intimacy & Relationships	JMS	—	—	S
Circles II: Stop Abuse	JMS	—	—	S/FS/V
Circles III: Safer Ways	JMS	—	—	S/V
Citizenship & the Law	JMS	—	—	S/V/FS
Communicate	THK	MS–HS	—	G
Communicate Expansion Cards	THK	MS–HS	—	G
Communicating Day By Day	HEL	JH	—	F
Communication Skills at Work: Customers	HEL	HS–AD	—	V
Communication Skills at Work: Supervisors	HEL	HS–AD	—	V
Communication Skills Series	SAD	C	2.6–2.8	B/W
Developing Functional English Skill Series: Letter Writing	MEM	MS–AD	—	W
Encyclopedia of Good Health	LCM	—	5.0–7.0	B
Family Living & Sex Education	GLO	—	—	W
Family Relationships	MEM	—	—	W
Getting Along with Others	EDM	EL	—	K
Good Neighbors	MEM	MS–AD	2.0–4.0	W
Guidance & Counseling Software	CNV	—	—	SW
High Interest Health	LCM	—	6.0–7.5	B
How to Manage Your Personal Affairs	SRA	MS–HS	2.4–4.0	W
How to Say No	EBS	MS–HS	—	K
How to Use the Telephone Book	SRA	MS–HS	2.5–5.0	W
How to Write Letters & Messages	SRA	MS–HS	2.4–4.0	W
Human Sexuality	EDM	—	—	TR
Improving Your Self Concept	ESW	JH–AD	3.0–4.0	SW
Job Survival Skills	HEL	HS–AD	—	V

RELATIONSHIPS *(continued)*

Material	Publisher	Age Level	Reading Level	Type
Job Awareness Kit	MEM	MS–AD	4.0	K
Job Challenges	MEM	HS–AD	2.0–4.0	W
Last Goodbye	FJA	JH–HS	2.5–4.0	W
Let's Have a Talk	FJA	MS–HS	2.8	W
Life Horizons I	JMS	—	—	S
Life Horizons II	JMS	—	—	S
Life Situations	LCM	—	2.0–3.5	B/DM
Life Skills Attitudes in Everyday Living	EDI	MS–AD	3.0–5.0	W
Life Skills Attitudes on the Job	EDI	MS–AD	3.0–5.0	W
LifeFacts 1	JMS	—	—	K
LifeFacts 2	JMS	—	—	K
LifeFacts 3	JMS	—	—	K
Living Alone	COM	HS–AD	3.0–4.0	SW
Marathon	JMS	—	—	K
Me & My Future	EDI	MS–HS	5.0–8.0	W
Me & Others	EDI	MS–HS	0–6.0	W
Mind Your Manners—Self-Confidence	JMS	—	—	V
Mind Your Manners—Social Success	JMS	—	—	V
Mr. & Ms.	FJA	HS	3.0–4.0	W
Now Is the Time	ESW	HS–AD	3.0–4.0	V
Now You're Talking	EAC	—	—	K
Pacemaker Communication Skills	HEL	—	2.0–3.0	W
Personal Health & Conduct	FJA	HS	—	FS/A
Personal Power	PRO	MS–HS	—	TR
Pouvant I	PRO	MS–HS	—	TR/B
PREP for Effective Family Living	AGS	HS	—	K
Prepare Curriculum	REP	JH–HS	—	TR
Put Down Pro	FJA	JH–HS	2.5–4.0	W
Real Friends	LCM	—	5.5–6.0	B
Real Life Reading Workshop	LCM	—	2.0–4.0	FC/DM
Refusal Skill Video	REP	JH–HS	—	B/V
Refusal Skills	REP	JH–HS	—	TR
Self-Advocacy for Persons with Developmental Disabilities	JMS	—	—	V
Sexuality Education for Persons with Severe Developmental Disabilities	JMS	—	—	S
Sharing an Apartment	FJA	JH–HS	2.5–4.0	W
Simply English	HIN	EL–AD	—	B/W
Skills for Living	REP	—	—	B
Skillstreaming the Adolescent	REP	MS–HS	—	B

RELATIONSHIPS *(continued)*

Material	Publisher	Age Level	Reading Level	Type
Skillstreaming Video	REP	MS–HS	—	B/V
Social Perceptual Training for Community Living	EAC	—	—	K
Social Skill Strategies—A	THK	MS–HS	5.0	B/DM
Social Skill Strategies—B	THK	MS–HS	6.0–7.0	B/DM
Take Charge of Your Life	LCM	—	4.0–4.5	W
TAWK	PEK	—	—	G
Teaching Behavioral Self-Control to Students	PRO	—	—	TR
Teenage Parents	LLS	HS	—	V
The Choice	FJA	JH–HS	2.5–4.0	W
The Dynamics of Relationships	EBS	MS–HS	—	B
The Power of Choice	CNV	—	—	V
The Promise	FJA	JH–HS	2.5–4.0	W
The Waksman Social Skills Curriculum	PRO	MS–HS	—	B/W
The Walker Social Skills Program	PRO	MS–HS	—	B/W
Time to Change	FJA	JH–HS	2.5–4.0	W
Tips	JMS	—	—	V/S
Walker Social Skills Curriculum: ACCEPTS Program	PRO	EL	—	B
Walker Social Skills Curriculum: ACCESS Program	PRO	JH–HS	—	B
What Could I Say?	REP	JH–HS	—	V
What You Should Know About Avoiding Rape & Sexual Assault in Federal Workplace	USG	—	—	P
Working I	JMS	—	—	V
Working II	JMS	—	—	V/T
Yes I Can . . . Work with People	REP	—	—	K
Your Personal Habits	ESW	HS–AD	4.0–5.0	SW
Your Work Habits	ESW	HS–AD	4.0–5.0	SW

PERSONAL EXPRESSION

Material	Publisher	Age Level	Reading Level	Type
Developing Functional English Skill Series: Letter Writing	MEM	MS–AD	—	W
Developing Functional English Skill Series: Writing for Your Life	MEM	MS–AD	—	W
English for Everyday Living	FJA	MS–HS	—	DM
Give Me a Call	FJA	MS–HS	2.8	W
Improving Your Self Concept	ESW	JH–AD	3.0–4.0	SW
Letter Writing	EDI	NS	2.0–3.0	W
Life Coping Skills Series: Forms & Messages	STV	MS–JH	2.0–4.0	W
Participating in Government	FJA	MS–HS	2.5	W
U.S. Postal Service 1990 National Five-Digit ZIP Code & Post Office Directory	USG	—	—	RB
Write Me a Note	FJA	MS–HS	2.8	W
Writing Friendly Letters, Business Letters, & Resumes	FJA	HS	—	A/W
Writing Notes and Letters	PEK	—	—	B

SELECTED MULTI-COMPONENT PROGRAMS

Material	Publisher	Age Level	Reading Level	Type
ABLEST-PLUS	FJA	JH–HS	1.0–3.0	CP
Becoming Independent	EDM	—	—	K
Books to Cope with Life's Challenges	SAD	MS–AD	2.3–4.0	W/B
Consume This Book for Life Skills	MEM	MS–AD	4.0	W
Consume This Book for Survival	MEM	MS–AD	4.0	W
Coping Workbook Series	SAD	HS–AD	1.0–4.0	W
In-Step	EBS	—	—	S/TR
Lessonmaker	EDM	—	—	SW
Life Centered Career Education	FJA	—	—	CP
Life Centered Career Education: A Competency Based Approach	CEC	—	—	TR
Life Centered Career Education: Activity Books I & II	CEC	—	—	TR
Life School Program	FJA	HS	1.0–4.0	CP
Life School Worktexts	FJA	MS–HS	3.5–5.0	CP
On Your Own	EDM	—	2.5	WB
Real-Life English	STV	AD	—	W
SCIL: Systematic Curriculum for Independent Living	ACT	HS–AD	—	TR
Shop Talk	REP	—	—	TR
Simply English	EBS	MS–AD	—	K
Stepping Out Cues	EDM	—	—	K
Struggle	EBS	MS–AD	—	G
Survival Guides	SAD	JH–AD	2.0–3.0	B/W
Survival Signs Sampler	ATT	—	—	SW
Survival Skills Resource Kit	EBS	—	—	K
Teaching Interpersonal and Community Living Skills	PRO	HS–AD	—	TR
Teaching Students Words to Live By	EDM	MS–AD	—	K
Teaching the Moderate and Severely Handicapped	PRO	—	—	TR

Publishers' Addresses

Able Net, Inc.
1081 Tenth Avenue S.E.
Minneapolis, MN 55414
(800) 322-0956 or
(612) 379-0956
Fax: (612) 379-9143

Academic Therapy Publications
20 Commercial Boulevard
Novato, CA 94949-6191
(800) 422-7249 or
(415) 883-3314

AGS
4201 Woodland Road
P.O. Box 99
Circle Pines, MN 55014-1796
(800) 328-2560
Fax: (612) 786-9077

Aspen Publishers, Inc.
7201 McKinney Circle
P.O. Box 990
Frederick, MD 21701-9782
(800) 638-8437

Attainment Company, Inc.
504 Commerce Parkway
Verona, WI 53593-1377
(800) 327-4269

Cambridge Development Lab, Inc.
214 Third Avenue
Waltham, MA 02154
(800) 637-0047 or
(617) 890-4640

Council for Exceptional Children
1920 Association Drive
Reston, VA 22091-1589
(703) 620-3660 or
Fax: (703) 264-9494

ComputAbility Corporation
40000 Grand River
Suite #109
Novi, MI 48050
(800) 433-8872 or
(313) 477-6720

Communication Skill Builders
3830 E. Bellevue
P.O. Box 42050-P2
Tucson, AZ 85733
(602) 323-7500
Fax: (602) 325-0306

The Conover Company Ltd.
P.O. Box 155
Omro, WI 54963
(800) 933-1933

Contemporary Books, Inc.
180 N. Michigan Avenue
Chicago, IL 60601
(800) 621-1918 or
(312) 782-9181

Cuisenaire Company
12 Church Street
Box D
New Rochelle, NY 10802
(800) 237-3142 or
(914) 235-0900
Fax: (914) 576-3480

Curriculum Associates, Inc.
5 Esquire Road
N. Billerica, MA 01862-2589
(800) 255-0248 or
(508) 667-8000
Fax: (508) 667-5706

Don Johnston Development Equipment, Inc.
P.O. Box 639
10000 N. Rand Road
Building 115
Wauconda, IL 60084-0639
(800) 999-4660
(708) 526-2682

EBSCO Curriculum Materials
Box 486
Birmingham, AL 35201
(800) 633-8623
Fax: (205) 991-1479

EdITS
P.O. Box 7234
San Diego, CA 92167
(619) 222-1666

Edmark
P.O. Box 3903
Bellevue, WA 98008-3903
(800) 426-0856

Educational Design, Inc.
47 W. 13th Street
New York, NY 10011
(800) 221-9372 or
(212) 255-7900

Educational Press
Department 9111
P.O. Box 32382
Baltimore, MD 21208-8382
(301) 561-5912

Educational Resources
1550 Executive Drive
Elgin, IL 60123
(800) 624-2926 or
(708) 888-8300
Fax: (708) 888-8300

Entry Publishing, Inc.
P.O. Box 20277
New York, NY 10025
(212) 662-9703

Exceptional Educational Software
Lawrence Productions, Inc.
1800 S. 35th Street
Galesburg, MI 49053
(800) 421-4157
(616) 665-7075
Fax: (616) 665-7060

Fearon/Janus/Quercus
500 Harbor Boulevard
Belmont, CA 94022
(800) 877-4283

Gamco Industries
P.O. Box 1862A34
Big Spring, TX 79721-1862
(800) 351-1404 or
(915) 267-6327
Fax: (915) 267-7480

Globe Book Company
Simon & Schuster
4350 Equity Drive
P.O. Box 2649
Columbus, OH 43216
(800) 848-9500

Harvest Educational Labs
73 Pelham Street
Newport, RI 02840
(401) 846-6580

High Noon Books
A Division of Academic Therapy Publications
20 Commercial Boulevard
Novato, CA 94949-6191
(800) 422-7249 or
(415) 883-3314

Lakeshore Curriculum Materials Company
2695 E. Dominguez Street
P.O. Box 6261
Carson, CA 90749
(800) 421-5354 or
(213) 537-8600
Fax: (213) 603-2991

Laureate Learning Systems, Inc.
110 E. Spring Street
Winooski, VT 05404
(800) 562-6801

Learning Resources Store
Ready Reference Press
P.O. Box 5249
Santa Monica, CA 90405
(800) 424-5627
or (213) 474-5175

LinguiSystems, Inc.
P.O. Box 747
3100 Fourth Avenue
East Moline, IL 61244
(800) PRO-IDEA

Magnetic Way
A Division of Creative Edge, Inc.
2495 N. Forest Road
Getzville, NY 14068
(800) 626-5052 or
(716) 689-1655
Fax: (716) 689-6712

Media Materials, Inc.
Department 910301
1821 Portal Street
Baltimore, MD 21224
(800) 638-1010 or
(301) 633-0730
Fax: (301) 633-2758

Peekan Publications
P.O. Box 513
Freeport, IL 61032
(800) 345-7335 or
(815) 235-9130

PRO-ED, Inc.
8700 Shoal Creek Boulevard
Austin, TX 78757-6897
(512) 451-3246
Fax: (512) 451-8542

Programming Concepts, Inc.
5221 McCullough
San Antonio, TX 78212
(210) 824-5949
(800) 594-4263
Fax: (512) 824-8055

Project Special Education
Box 31
Sauk Centre, MN 56378-0031
(800) 255-0752
Fax: (612) 352-6750

Research Press
Department E
Box 3177
Champaign, IL 61826
(217) 352-3273

RPM Press, Inc.
P.O. Box 31483
Tucson, AZ 85751-1483
(602) 886-1990

Saddleback Educational, Inc.
711 W. 17th Street, Suite F-12
Costa Mesa, CA 92627
(714) 650-4010
Fax: (714) 650-1108

Software for Education
P.O. Box 12947
San Rafael, CA 94913-2947
(800) 521-6263

SRA
Macmillan/McGraw-Hill
155 N. Wacker Drive
Chicago, IL 60606
(800) 621-0476
Fax: (312) 984-7935

James Stanfield Publishing Company
P.O. Box 41058-T
Santa Barbara, CA 93140
(800) 421-6534
Fax: (805) 565-3918

Steck-Vaughn
P.O. Box 26015
Austin, TX 78755
(800) 531-5015
Fax: (512) 343-6854

Sunburst Communications
39 Washington Avenue
Pleasantville, NY 10570-9971
(800) 431-1934 or
(914) 769-5030 (call collect)

Thinking Publications
1731 Westgate Road
P.O. Box 163
Eau Claire, WI 54702-0163
(800) 225-GROW

U.S. Government Books
710 North Capitol Street NW
Washington, DC 20401
(202) 275-2091

VGM Career Horizons
4255 W. Touhy Avenue
Lincolnwood, IL 60646-1975
(800) 323-4900
(312) 679-5500

Potential Field Experience Sites and Speakers

SCHOOL-BASED FIELD EXPERIENCES

All schools provide a readily available opportunity to observe and practice life skills on campus. A listing of all job experiences available on a particular campus provides a starting point for the teacher to make contacts among the school staff for inclusion in the program. On-campus field experiences provide the best "first" experience to prepare students for off-campus encounters. When setting up the on-campus field experiences, follow the same procedures you would use for off-campus field experiences. The Community Resource Person(s) and the Field Experience documents in Appendix D and Appendix E, respectively, provide those guidelines.

Sample people/locations on campus include secretary, bookkeeper, cook, cafeteria workers, building engineer, janitor, groundskeeper, clerical staff, principal, teachers, counselors, social workers, and school psychologist. The number and types of positions will vary from campus to campus.

COMMUNITY FIELD EXPERIENCE POSSIBILITIES

The availability of possible field experiences will vary in each community, so the following list of sug-

gestions is far from exhaustive; it is meant to be a starting point for teachers. Local lists will reflect the uniqueness of each community.

Businesses

car dealerships
hardware stores
drug stores/pharmacies
grocery stores
department/discount stores
catalog stores
bakeries
restaurants (sit-down)
restaurants (fast food)
plant nurseries
florists
banks
construction company sites
photographers
bookstores
gas stations (full- and self-service)
auto repair/body shops
printing/copy companies
computer companies/stores
tax preparation services
real estate/apartment locators
Better Business Bureau
Chamber of Commerce

(continued on next page)

independent living centers
group homes

Health Resources

hospitals
doctor/dentist offices
Red Cross centers
ophthalmologist/optometrist/optician
veterinarian/veterinary clinic

Local Government

city hall
utility companies (gas, electricity, water, telephone)
recycling centers
public library
police department/drug-abuse prevention program
fire department
transit company
courthouse
voter registration office

State Government

highway patrol
state legislators' local offices
state capitol
department of motor vehicles
employment office
unemployment office
vocational rehabilitative office

Federal Government

post office
IRS office
Social Security Administration Office
criminal courthouse
senators' and representatives' local offices

Media

newspaper office
radio stations

TV stations
cable company
weather station
other publications (e.g., locally published magazines)

Leisure Options

plays
movies
concerts (classical, pop, rock, etc.)
museums (art, historical, science, etc.)
YMCA/YWCA
shopping malls
bowling alleys
parks
skating rinks
video arcades
expositions/special events (home, car, boat shows; circus; county/state fairs, etc.)
sporting events
interest clubs (sports, chess, environmental, etc.)

Education

colleges/universities
community colleges
vocational technical schools
daycare centers/preschools

Transportation

airport
train station
bus station
transit company
cab companies
ferries

SPEAKERS

The following list represents a sample of the speakers available in most communities. Many of these individuals and their businesses visit schools as a community service and are most willing to do what they can to educate the public about their jobs and how their businesses function. In addition, they recognize the value of visiting schools and enlightening prospective employees about the types of jobs their businesses offer. Again, teachers need to create their own list that reflects their own communities. These are offered as a starting point.

League of Women Voters
attorney
police office/sheriff
apartment locator
telephone company representative
realtor
insurance agent
vocational rehabilitation counselor
drug-abuse prevention counselor
local business owner
health care provider (nurse, technician,
    doctor, dentists, etc.)
travel agent
representatives of various national health
    organizations (Heart Association,
    American Diabetes Association, etc.)
director of independent living center or
    group home
local, state, and federal judges

COMMUNITY SERVICE ORGANIZATIONS

The following community service organizations will usually offer speakers to discuss the organization's function and purpose. In addition, many of them have facilities that may be used as a field experience for your class.

YMCA/YWCA
Red Cross
League of Women Voters
American Legion
Veterans of Foreign Wars
Salvation Army
Urban League

CIVIC CLUBS

Civic clubs have various purposes. Some educate the public about various needs (e.g., Lion's Clubs educate the public about maintaining eyesight). Others offer financial assistance to schools, educational programs, and other needy groups. Many of these groups will offer financial support to a specific program, such as assisting with the expenses of a field experience's transportation, entrance fees, and meals. In addition, some civic clubs will provide assistance in acquiring materials by either purchasing them or helping to gather them in the community. Contact the various organizations for support in your local community.

Chamber of Commerce
Jaycees
Rotary Clubs
Kiwanis
Elks
Lions Club
Telephone Pioneers
Knights of Columbus

FINANCIAL CONSIDERATIONS FOR SUPPORTING FIELD EXPERIENCES

Implementing a field experience component can involve some expense. Many times money is needed for public transportation (buses, streetcars, trains, ferries, subways, etc.) even though special photo identification can usually be acquired from public transit for students with disabilities for reduced or free passage. In some communities, public transportation is not available, so other forms of transportation must be used. This can involve money that may not be available. The following activities have been used by classes and schools to raise money, alleviating some (if not all) of a field experience's expenses. This list is not exhaustive; it is meant as a suggestion list to get you started. In addition, many of the previously listed civic clubs will sponsor the field experience programs of local schools, special programs, or individual classes.

- weekly bake sales during school lunch or at special events
- selling individualized computer-generated greeting cards during holiday periods (Halloween, Christmas, Valentine's Day, etc.)

- providing services for the faculty (washing cars, running errands during field experiences, etc.)
- obtaining special discounts from stores, movie theaters, food establishments, etc.
- selling candy
- selling concessions at school events (sports games, plays, special programs, etc.)
- selling school supplies
- maintaining a recycling program
- organizing game tournaments (Monopoly, Scrabble, chess, etc.)

Preparing for a Community Resource Person's Visit

Prepare Yourself

1. Determine the instructional goals of your class and how the resource person can help you achieve them.

2. Study the resource person's field so that you will be informed about what they do. You might ask them to send you some materials about their job, business, agency, or hobby.

3. Think of some questions or topics of discussion that may be of interest to your students.

4. Be prepared to support the resource person in the classroom.

Prepare Your Students

1. Share with the students the resource person's experience and expertise in the area they are studying.

2. Make sure that the class interest is developed—that is your job, not the resource person's.

3. Brainstorm with your students to develop a list of questions for the resource person.

4. Have the students discuss appropriate behavior.

5. Have materials, displays, or projects available to share with the resource person.

Prepare Your Resource Person

1. Inform the resource person of what the instructional goals for the class are and what you want the students to do.

2. Share with the resource person information such as the size of your class, the age of your students, and amounts of preparation for this topic.

3. Send a reminder to the resource person concerning time, date, location of school, and phone number where you can be reached. Inquire about any needs they may have.

4. Encourage the resource person(s) to do something other than simply lecture. Suggest they wear their work clothes, bring some tools of the trade, publications, handouts, slides, videos, or other items that would be of interest to your students.

Other Things to Prepare For

1. Media needs

2. Someone to greet the resource person

3. Break time

4. Unknown factors: a boring speaker, a no-show, or an inappropriate presentation

5. Notifying other teachers and the principal

6. If appropriate, invite other interested students, teachers, etc.

Afterwards:

For the Students

- Discuss the presentation and relate it to the concepts being studied.

- Ask the students to evaluate the presentation, both in writing and in discussion.

- Plan a follow-up activity that will enable the students to study the concept more or put them into action.

- Ask students to write thank-you notes to the resource person(s).

For the Resource Person

- Personally thank the resource person, verbally, and follow up with a written note.

- Inform them of the positive feedback from the student evaluation.

For the Teacher

- Establish a file of resource persons, student evaluations, and follow-up activities.

- Note anything you would do differently next time.

Adapted from "The Resource Person," developed and prepared by Roxy Smarzik, Instructional Services Department, Region X Education Services Center, Richardson, Texas.

Preparing for a Field Experience

Prepare Yourself

- Determine why you want to go. How does the field experience fit into your instructional goals?

- Visit the site before the field experience. Talk with the people there to tailor the trip for your students, class content, and instructional goals.

Prepare Your Students

- Explain the purpose of the field experience and how it relates to their class work.

- Ask for their input concerning what they hope to see and what they think they will see.

- Identify on-site points of interest to anticipate.

- Explain and identify proper field experience behavior. Let students know what you expect from them.

Prepare the Site

- Consult with the site managers/directors about your intended field experiences. Plan to have them meet the group. Ask if personnel will be available for a tour.

- Inform them of your instructional goals and the focus of your curriculum.

- Follow up with a confirmation note.

Complete Your Preparations

Take care of details such as administrative approval, parental notification/approval, transportation, bus passes, chaperons, notifying other teachers, lunch plans, restroom stops, and scheduling. Certain field experiences or guest speakers may spark activity in numerous directions. Depending on your instructional goals, any resource lends itself to multiple exploration. For example, a field experience at a a supermarket or department store could involve the following topics:

1. Product comparison
2. Weights and measures
3. Transportation of materials
4. Budgeting
5. Product display
   a. Picture making
   b. Collage, mobiles, murals
   c. Food or clothing design and packaging
6. Store design
   a. Architecture
   b. Floor layout
7. Store location
8. Selection and varieties of products
9. Price comparison
10. Jobs available/application procedures
11. Departments
    a. Product
    b. Accounting
    c. Advertising
    d. Management

While You're There

- Supplement your guide's information at the site by relating what the students see to their class activities.

- Offer the students different ways of viewing and experiencing the trip. Design an on-site activity (e.g., price comparison); assign them to interview a person while they are there, or ask one student to be the on-site reporter.

- Encourage direct experiences. Students enjoy wearing hard hats or lab coats. Demonstrations are a refreshing change from the lecture approach.

- Keep on schedule and watch your time!

- Make sure the group acts as a team with the same goals.

- Assign a student to photograph the trip. Pictures could be useful for a review of the trip.

After You Return

- Have students write a thank-you note to appropriate individuals at the site.

- Have students evaluate the field experience. Compare student expectations before and after the trip.

- Plan a follow-up activity that will enable students to apply what they learned both in school and on-site.

- Keep a file of field experiences with information about location, contact people, evaluation, and follow-up activities. Note anything you would do differently next time.

Adapted from "The Field Trip," developed and prepared by Roxy Smarzik, Instructional Services Department, Region X Education Services Center, Richardson, Texas.

Sample Field Experience Checklists

These field experience checklists were adapted from the St. Bernard Parish (Louisiana) School System Alternative Program. We wish to give special acknowledgment to Deborah Lord and Kathy Wendling for sharing this information.

FIELD EXPERIENCE CHECKLIST
Register to Vote at the Police Jury Building

NAME: _____ DATE: _____

	A	NA
1. Dresses appropriately	_____	_____
2. Brings appropriate personal information	_____	_____
3. Walks on sidewalks	_____	_____
4. Has correct change for the bus	_____	_____
5. Presents bus card to driver and places money in change receptacle	_____	_____
6. Politely asks for voter registration forms to fill out	_____	_____
7. Completes form with little or no assistance	_____	_____
8. Selects and orders items from Ed and Mike's Mexican Cantina	_____	_____
9. Uses appropriate table manners	_____	_____
10. Leaves appropriate tip for the server	_____	_____
11. Rings bell at the appropriate stop	_____	_____
12. Waits for bus to move before crossing the street	_____	_____

GRADE: _____

COMMENTS:

_____

_____

_____

_____

FIELD EXPERIENCE CHECKLIST
Using Public Transportation

NAME: _____ DATE: _____

	A	NA
1. Dressed appropriately	_____	_____
2. Gives coupons to the bus driver	_____	_____
3. Gives correct change for city bus	_____	_____
4. Places change in receptacle	_____	_____
5. Asks driver for transfer	_____	_____
6. Walks on sidewalks when available	_____	_____
7. Pushes tape at appropriate stop	_____	_____
8. Gets off the bus and waits until bus passes before crossing the street	_____	_____

GRADE: _____

COMMENTS:

_____

_____

_____

_____

FIELD EXPERIENCE CHECKLIST
Don's Wholesale Club
Comparison Shopping

NAME: _____ DATE: _____

	A	NA
1. Appropriate dress: Collared shirt; Jeans in good condition	_____	_____
2. Clean shaven	_____	_____
3. Well-groomed hair, nails, and ears	_____	_____
4. Smells nice	_____	_____
5. Makes polite conversation	_____	_____
6. Refrains from name-calling	_____	_____
7. Talks in a soft voice	_____	_____
8. Does comparison shopping in an orderly manner	_____	_____
9. Handles equipment (TV, stereos, VCRs) with care	_____	_____
10. Orders in a clear voice at Bill's Famous Hamburgers	_____	_____
11. Says "thank you" after ordering	_____	_____
12. Uses appropriate table manners	_____	_____
13. Waits for everyone to finish eating before getting up to leave	_____	_____
14. Cleans up table after eating	_____	_____
15. Returns to the bus at the right time	_____	_____

GRADE: _____

COMMENTS:

_____

_____

_____

_____

Sample ITP Formats

STATE OF HAWAII
DEPARTMENT OF EDUCATION

INDIVIDUALIZED TRANSITION PLAN

Student's Name _____ Birthdate: _____
                     Last   First   M.I.

School _____ Student's   ITP Conference
                                         I.D. # _____ _____ _____ Date _____

IPP/Diploma: _____ Passed HSTEC: _____ Projected Graduation Year: _____

Social   Work   State   Health
Security # _____ Permit _____ ID _____ Certificate _____

PARTICIPANTS:

Name   Position

_____   _____

_____   _____

_____   _____

_____   _____

_____   _____

_____   _____

_____   _____

_____   _____

_____   _____

_____   _____

STATEMENT OF DISCLAIMER

The ITP is not intended to be a contract. It represents a suggested plan to facilitate a person's transition into adulthood. Services provided by certain agencies indicated in the plan may not always be available or may be subject to qualification requirements. Furthermore, some agencies may require a fee or fees for services provided. In such instances, the parents or legal guardians may be required to assume financial responsibility for such services.

6/90, RS 90-8070

TRANSITION SERVICE AREAS	PERSON/AGENCY RESPONSIBLE	TIMELINE		COMMENTS
		Initiation Date	Completion Date	
A. Vocational/Educational Goal:				
B. Community Goal:				
C. Home and Family Goal:				

PERSON(S) RESPONSIBLE: F-Family S-School A-Agency ST-Students
COMMENTS: I-Initiated C-Completed R-Revised O-Others

TRANSITION SERVICE AREAS	PERSON/AGENCY RESPONSIBLE	TIMELINE		COMMENTS
		Initiation Date	Completion Date	
D. Recreation/Leisure Goal:				
E. Financial Support Goal:				
F. Health Goal:				
G. Transportation Goal:				

PERSON(S) RESPONSIBLE: F-Family   S-School   A-Agency   ST-Students
COMMENTS: I-Initiated   C-Completed   R-Revised   O-Others

STATE OF HAWAII
DEPARTMENT OF EDUCATION
INDIVIDUALIZED TRANSITION PLAN
PROGRAM REVIEW

PARTICIPANTS: Review Date _____

Name   Position   Phone Nos.

_____   _____

_____   _____

_____   _____

_____   _____

_____   _____

_____   _____

_____   _____

_____   _____

_____   _____

PARTICIPANTS: Review Date _____

Name   Position   Phone Nos.

_____   _____

_____   _____

_____   _____

_____   _____

_____   _____

_____   _____

_____   _____

_____   _____

_____   _____

PARTICIPANTS: Review Date _____

Name   Position   Phone Nos.

_____   _____

_____   _____

_____   _____

_____   _____

_____   _____

_____   _____

_____   _____

_____   _____

_____   _____

Santa Fe Public Schools Special Education Services
Individual Transition Plan
(Attachment-to IEP, Grades 8–12)

Date of Meeting: _____ School: _____

Student Name: _____ D.O.B. _____ Grade: ____

I. Graduation Plan (check one):

( ) Standard Plan (23 required credits & pass NMHS Competency Exam)

( ) Modified Plan (IEP Graduation as per district policy)

( ) Certificate of Completion (complete planned course of study)

Anticipated Date of High School Graduation: _____

II. Need (check one):

( ) The Transition Team has determined that this student is not in need of special transition services/support beyond what is available to all students in the public school.

( ) The Transition Team has determined that this student is in need of special transition services and/or support.

III. Transition Services/Support Needs (check each area that applies):

( ) Vocational Assessment   ( ) Employment

( ) Career/Vocational Guidance   ( ) Medical

( ) Career Vocational Education   ( ) Transportation/Mobility

( ) Residential/Independent Living   ( ) Leisure/Recreation

( ) Socialization/Community Integration   ( ) Income Support

( ) Postsecondary Education   ( ) Guardianship/Advocacy
    (Academic/Vocational)

                                                ( ) Other: _____

Transition Area	Goals and Objectives (Actions to be taken)	Responsible Persons Parent/School/Agency	Time Line

Sample Permission Letters

The sample letters were adapted from the St. Bernard School System (Louisiana). We wish to give special acknowledgment to Deborah Lord for sharing this information.

DATE _____

Dear Parents:

Our class will be visiting the _____

on _____. The purpose of the

field experience is to _____.

We will/will not be eating lunch off campus. We will be eating

lunch at _____.

Students will need $_____ for lunch.

We will be using _____ for transportation.

Students will need $_____ for transportation.

Please sign below, giving your permission for your son/daughter to participate in this field experience.

Thank you for your continued support of our field experience.

Sincerely,

Teacher

_____

My son/daugher _____ has my permission to participate in but not be limited to the following activities:

    (activity) _____

    (activity) _____

    (activity) _____

Parent's Signature: _____

Parent's Name (Printed): _____

April 1, 1993

Dear Parents:

On Thursday, April 22, 1993, our class will be going to visit Maureen's Cleaners on Genoa St. The purpose of this trip is to identify the service(s) offered by Maureen's and explore the employment options offered by this local business.

The students will be required to wear regular school clothes. We will eat lunch while we are out. Please send at least $5.00 for lunch at Helen's Pizza Palace.

We will be taking public transportation. Bus coupons will be provided. The class will return to school before the last bell rings.

Please sign below, giving your permission for your son/daughter to attend this field experience.

Thank you for your continued support of our field experiences.

Sincerely,

Kathie A. Conwell

_____

My son/daugher _____ has my permission to participate in but not be limited to the following activities:

    —visit Maureen's Cleaners
    —have lunch at Helen's Pizza Palace
    —ride public transportation

Parent's Signature: _____

Parent's Name (Printed): _____

November 4, 1993

Dear Parents:

We will be visiting Colleen's Factory Outlet Mall on Thursday, December 9, 1993. The purpose of the trip will be to compare prices of items found on the trip to those at Pat's Closet.

Students will need at least $8.00 for the buffet-style lunch at John and Joe's Buffet. All students will be given ample time to shop if they bring money to do so.

Public transportation will be used. The students must bring their RTA photo ID and 20 cents for the discounted fare. If they do not bring these items they will have to pay the full adult fare of $1.10.

Please sign below, giving your permission for your son/daughter to participate in this field experience.

Thank you for your continued support of our class field experiences.

Sincerely,

Bridgid Newman

_____

My son/daugher _____ has my permission to participate in but not be limited to the following activities:

     —comparison shopping at Colleen's Factory Outlet Mall
     —lunch at John and Joe's Buffet
     —riding public transportation

Parent's Signature: _____

Parent's Name (Printed): _____

Annotated Resource List

The following books, book chapters, and journal articles are sources of information on topics related to components of life skills that include, but are not limited to, adolescent/adult services, transition, employment of individuals with disabilities, Individual Transition Plans, independent living, life-long learning, vocational training, career education, rehabilitation, secondary special education, and work adjustment.

BOOKS

Brolin, D. E. (Ed.). (1991). *Life centered career education: A competency based approach.* Reston, VA: Council for Exceptional Children.

This guide focuses on the three curriculum areas of daily living, personal-social, and occupational skills. The competency units and assessment instrument are helpful in the development of a student's IEP.

Clark, G., & Kolstoe, O. P. (1990). *Career development and transition education for adolescents with disabilities.* Boston: Allyn & Bacon.

This book presents a model that attempts to broaden the choices students with special needs have in high school. The book focuses on secondary school programming at the high school level that addresses the students' needs for preparation after they leave the system. Topics such as student participation in programs, assessment, prevocational and occupational programming, job placement/training, interagency linkages, and transition are discussed.

Derman-Sparks, L., & the A.B.C. Task Force. (1989). *Anti-bias curriculum: Tools for empowering young children.* Washington, DC: National Association for the Education of Young Children.

This book outlines a guideline for developing an anti-bias curriculum, which embraces an educational philosophy as well as specific techniques and content. It asks teachers and children to confront troublesome issues rather than cover them up. An anti-bias perspective is integral to all aspects of daily classroom life. Specific titles include: Creating an Anti-Bias Environment, Learning About Racial Differences, Learning About Disability, Learning About Gender Identity, Learning About Cultural Differences, Learning to Resist Stereotyping and Discriminatory Behavior, Holiday Activities in an Anti-Bias Curriculum, Working With Parents, and Why an Anti-Bias Curriculum?

Higher Education and Adult Training for People with Disabilities (HEATH). (1988). *How to choose a college: Guide for the student with a disability.* Washington, DC: HEATH Resource Center.

A joint project of HEATH and the Association on Higher Education (formerly Association on Handicapped Student Services Programs in Post-Secondary Education—AHSSPPE), this guide provides guidance for individuals with learning disabilities on various aspects of choosing a college (services, support systems, adaptations, etc.).

Ianacone, R. A., & Stodden, R. A. (1987). *Transition issues and directions.* Reston, VA: Division on Mental Retardation–Council for Exceptional Children.

This monograph is a collection of 12 chapters addressing the various phases of transition for differing ages and levels of mental retardation. The second part of the book relates the various perspectives of those individuals, schools, employers, and agencies who participate in the transition process. Viewpoints of the following are given: special education, vocational education, vocational rehabilitation, community services, parent advocacy, and employment.

Ludlow, B. L., Turnbull, A. P., & Luckasson, R. (1988). *Transitions to adult life for people with mental retardation: Principles and practices.* Baltimore, MD: Paul H. Brookes.

This book focuses on transition issues of individuals with mental retardation. The principles and practices of transition programming are described. This book is intended to offer suggestions for designing, implementing, and evaluating transition programs for "real people in real communities."

Mannix, D. (1992). *Life skills activities for special children.* West Nyack, NY: Center for Applied Research in Education.

This is a collection of 145 life skills lessons. The lessons are organized into the following areas: basic survival skills, personal independence, community independence, and getting along with others. Included are reproducible line master worksheets and parent letters.

McClure, L., Cook, S., & Thompson, V. (1977). *Experience-based learning: How to make the community your classroom.* Portland, OR: Northwest Regional Educational Laboratory.

This book contains volumes of information for those interested in setting up their community as a primary learning environment. Focus of experience-based learning combines four major capabilities: (a) community involvement, (b) individualized instruction, (c) guidance, and (d) staff as managers of learning. Topics include structuring the learning process, linking community resources with student projects, locating resource persons, and managing the process.

Retish, P., Hitchings, W., Horvath, M., & Schmalle, B. (1991). *Students with mild disabilities in the secondary school.* New York: Longman.

This book gives readers assistance in developing curriculum, identifying strategies, and delivering instruction in academic, career, and life skills at the secondary level. Issues regarding transition of adolescents with special needs to postsecondary settings is a consideration that appears throughout the book.

Schieber, B., & Talpers, J. (1987). *Unlocking potential: College and other choices for learning disabled people.* Bethesda, MD: Alder & Alder.

A guide for students with learning disabilities to achieve access to postsecondary environments. Discussion of available options, how to select an appropriate one, and how to achieve campus access through academic advising, accommodations, study skills, and personal adjustment.

Schloss, P. J., Smith, M. A., & Schloss, C. N. (1990). *Instructional methods for adolescents with learning and behavior problems.* Boston: Allyn & Bacon.

This book describes methods that can be used effectively in promoting skills that are necessary for postsecondary situations. Topics include an educational perspective on secondary education, general instructional methods, and instruction in basic and functional skills.

West, L. L., Corbey, S., Boyer-Stephens, A., Jones, B., & Sarkees-Wircenski, M. (1992). *Integrating transition planning into the IEP process.* Reston, VA: Division on Career Development, Council for Exceptional Children.

This book focuses on various aspects of transition planning. Specific topics covered include integrating transition planning into a student's IEP, self-advocacy, assessment, curriculum, support services, interagency cooperation, and program evaluation and follow-up.

Siegel, S., Robert, M., Greener, K., Meyer, G., Halloran, W., & Gaylord-Ross, R. (1993). *Career ladders for challenged youths in transition from school to adult life.* Austin, TX: PRO-ED.

This book shares a successful program used in various school systems in California. The program focuses on issues related to effective transition for all students. Topics addressed include six principles of effective transition programming, the community classroom, the employability workshop, postsecondary services, developing sites for community classrooms, and history of transition.

CHAPTERS IN BOOKS

Cronin, M. E. (1988). Applying curriculum for the instruction of life skills. In G. A. Robinson, J. R. Patton, E. A. Polloway, & L. R. Sargent, *Best Practices in Mild Mental Disabilities Vol. II* (pp. 39–52). Des Moines, IA: Department of Public Instruction.

This chapter focuses on the importance of including life skills instruction in special education programs. Highlights include discussion of the Adult Performance Level (APL) Project as adapted for special needs populations, community instruction, and inclusion of non-traditional materials in the program.

Mastropieri, M. A., & Scruggs, T. (1987). Teaching for transition: Life skills, career, and vocational education. In M. Mastropieri & T. Scruggs, *Effective instruction for special education* (pp. 337–356). Austin, TX: PRO-ED.

This book provides practical information that is helpful to classroom teachers who work with students with mild disabilities. The authors have given practical information in both academic areas (reading, language arts, mathematics, science, social studies, and social skills). They have also shared information on teacher effectiveness, instructional design, evaluation, classroom management, social skills, transition, and consulting.

Patton, J. R., Cronin, M. E., Polloway, E. A., Hutchinson, D., & Robinson, B. A. (1989). Curricular considerations: A life skills orientation. In G. A. Robinson, J. R. Patton, E. A. Polloway, & L. R. Sargent, *Best practices in Mild Mental Disabilities* (pp. 23–37). Reston, VA: The Division on Mental Retardation of the Council for Exceptional Children.

This chapter discusses development of appropriate curriculum for secondary students with mild mental retardation and placement/environment options. Different curricular orientations are reviewed. A life skills approach (in particular Adult Performance Level Curriculum) is supported and discussed at length. Adult domains and demands are explained.

Wiederholt, J. L., & Wolffe, K. E. (1990). Preparing problem learners for independent living. In D. D. Hammill and N. R. Bartell, *Teaching students with learning and behavior problems* (pp. 451–503). Austin, TX: PRO-ED.

This chapter focuses on the areas in which students need preparation for life after high school. Discussions cover independent living skills, an overview of commonly used assessment techniques, and the teaching programs and activities used to strengthen independent living skills.

JOURNAL ARTICLES

Conant, C., & Weikart, N. (1990). Life skills grant introduces young adults to the rest of the library. *Public Libraries, 29,* 215–219.

The library is utilized by teen parents and non-college-bound students. Conant and Weikart designed their program to show students what a resource library can be and how it can meet their specific needs.

Cronin, M. E., Lord, D. C., & Wendling, K. (1991). Learning for life: The life skills curriculum. *Intervention in School and Clinic, 26,* 306–311.

This article presents the processes involved in creating and implementing a real-life curriculum. A school system in Louisiana is monitored as it attempts this feat. Adult Performance Level Curriculum is also discussed.

Cronin, M. E., Patton, J. R., & Polloway, E. A. (1991). Preparing for adult outcomes: A model for developing a life skills curriculum. Unpublished manuscript.

This article concerns the quality of secondary special education curriculum. The curricular considerations section addresses program types, guidelines for change, and adult-oriented models. A model for developing life skills curricula is outlined using life demands and adult domains in a top-down approach. Guidelines for implementation of this program are also discussed.

Dowdy, C., & Smith, T. E. C. (1991). Future based assessment and intervention. *Intervention in School and Clinic, 27,* 101–106.

This article concerns a smooth exit into the adult world for persons with disabilities. The seven steps of future based assessment and intervention are examined in depth.

Edgar, E. (1987). Secondary programs in special education: Are many of them justifiable? *Exceptional Children, 53,* 555–561.

The post school prospects for special education students are reviewed and discussed in-depth. The data presented are the force behind the author's recommendation, which would be a radical swing in secondary special education from traditional academics to functional academics.

Edgar, E. (1988). Transition from school to community. *Teaching Exceptional Children, 20,* 73–75.

This article provides examples of promising transition programs throughout the country. The article's introduction discussed interactions between agencies and important considerations in transition planning. Programs in Oregon, Minnesota, and New York are discussed.

Edgar, E. (1988). Employment as an outcome for mildly handicapped students: Current status and future directions. *Focus on Exceptional Children, 21,* 1–8.

The author reviews the poor state of employment for students with mild handicaps as well as programmatic options for improvement. Background discussion includes population characteristics, what the purpose of special education for this population should be, and a review of employment data. Presented solutions include building up vocational education teaching strategies and problem solving, as well as mentors and alternatives to high school.

Edgar, E. (1990). Is it time to change our view of the world? *Beyond Behavior, 1,* 9–13.

The condition of special education services and the future of special education students is debated. Edgar discusses specific findings in his own research and suggests ways to improve the situation.

Edgar, E. (1991). Providing ongoing support and making appropriate placements: An alternative to transition planning for mildly handicapped students. *Preventing School Failure, 35,* 36–39.

An alternative to typical secondary education is presented. Support for typical education such as tutors, counselors, and mentors are also discussed. Monitoring past "graduation" or program exit is suggested. Finally, guidelines are presented for making immediate best practice changes in secondary education for students with disabilities.

Elkins, N., & Elksnin, L. K. (1991). Facilitating the vocational success of students with mild handicaps. *The Journal for Vocational Special Needs Education, 13,* 5–11.

This article stresses the need for more social skills training in secondary special education. Commercially available social skills curricula for adolescents are reviewed and critiqued, and suggestions are made.

Fay, N., & Tsairides, C. (1989). Metric Mall. *Arithmetic Teacher, 37,* 6–11.

This science and math unit was designed to expose students to new situations that could transfer learning from the classroom to real life. Different stores were created with different skills to be practiced in each. Students would approach problems as consumers or shopkeepers. Examples are given.

Halpern, A. S., & Benz, M. R. (1987). A statewide examination of secondary special education for students with mild disabilities: Implications for the high school curriculum. *Exceptional Children, 54,* 122–129.

The study reported findings in a survey that was given to parents, administrators, and high school special education teachers. Subjects were asked to comment on the current status of secondary-level special education, existing gaps in programs, and what areas need improvement. Results showed discrepancies between professional and parental responses, and availability and utilization of services.

Hasazi, S. B., Gordon, L. R., & Roe, C. A. (1985). Factors associated with the employment status of handicapped youth exiting high school from 1979 to 1983. *Exceptional Children, 51,* 455–469.

Follow-up of 462 students who had received special education services and were interviewed for this research, which sought to gain information on current employment. Employment and training history and use of social services are covered. Results revealed that more than half of the sample was employed, most found work through personal networks, and working during high school favorably affected employment. Additional relationships to employment were noted and discussed. These include gender, location, manner of exiting high school, vocational education and service-agency contact.

Mithaug, D. E., Horiuchi, C. N., & Fanning, P. N. (1975). A report on the Colorado statewide follow up survey of special education students. *Exceptional Children, 51,* 397–404.

This study sought to conduct a follow-up study of special education students who had graduated from high school. A total of 234 students were interviewed and asked to comment on background information, school experiences, and job or school experiences after graduation.

Mittler, H., & Buckingham, A. (1987). Getting ready to leave. *British Journal of Special Education, 14,* 11–13.

A study that involved weekly group sessions on life skills is presented. The process for development of the method is discussed. Students participated in choosing content, games, and role-playing. Suggestions for conducting a group are given.

Murphy, S., & Walsh, J. (1989). Economics and the real-life connection. *Social Studies and the Young Learner, 2,* 6–8.

Economics is presented as a means of practicing decision making and recognizing responsibility. Basic economic concepts and how they apply to everyday activities are discussed.

Neubert, D. A., & Foster, J. (1988). Learning disabled students make the transitions. *Teaching Exceptional Children, 20,* 24–44.

This article outlines a guide to help educators assist learning disabled individuals in exploring employment and postsecondary options and to enhance transition. The program outlined (Community-Based Exploration Guide) involves five steps: developing an employability profile; identifying areas to explore; community exploration; summarizing and implementing; seeking the information a student needs to achieve his or her goals for employment or postsecondary education.

Polloway, E. A., Patton, J. R., Epstein, M. H., & Smith, T. E. C. (1989). Comprehensive curriculum for students with mild handicaps. *Focus on Exceptional Children, 21,* 1–12.

This article examines main facets of developing curriculum for students with mild handicaps, namely: evaluation of models, selection and needs of subgroups in this population. The model orientations discussed are academic or social remediation, maintenance through tutor or learning strategies, and emphasizing functional skills. Issues in designing curricula are highlighted.

Polloway, E. A., Patton, J. R., Smith, J. D., & Rodrique, T. W. (1991). Issues in program design for elementary students with mild retardation: Emphasis on curriculum, development. *Education and Training in Mental Retardation, 26,* 142–150.

The focus of this paper is on instructional program design with emphasis on curriculum for elementary students who are mildly retarded. Vertical transitions (preschool, middle school) and horizontal transitions (integration) are discussed. The authors support a "subsequent environments as attitudes" approach.

VanBuren, J. B. (1989). Documentation of basic skills in consumer and homemaking education curriculum. *Journal of Vocational Home Economics Education, 7,* 37–45.

This study attempts to demonstrate that basic skills included in academic curriculum are also included in and made functional by homemaking curriculum. The results showed correlations between the two curricula, especially in the language arts and social studies curricula.

Wiggins, S. B., & Behrmann, N. N. (1989). Increasing independence through community learning. *Teaching Exceptional Children, 21,* 20–24.

This article supports extending the classroom into real world settings. The program presented has components dealing with transportation, safety, grocery stores, and restaurants. The author elaborates upon these components.

Wircenski, J. L., & Sarkees, M. D. (1990). Instructional alternatives: Rescue strategies for at-risk students. *NASSP Curriculum Report, 19,* 1–6.

This article focuses on preventing high school dropout. Characteristics of successful programs are presented in depth. Examples of well-designed programs across the country are given.

Professional Journals/ Periodicals

The following publications are sources of information on topics related to life skills components including but not limited to adolescent/adult services, employment of individuals with disabilities, transition, Individual Transition Plans, independent living, lifelong learning, vocational training, career education, rehabilitation, secondary special education, and work adjustment.

Adult Learning
   1112 16th Street NW
   Suite 420
   Washington, DC 20036
   (202) 463-6333

Adult Basic Education Journal
   Commission on Adult Basic Education
   Box 592053
   Orlando, FL 32859-2053
   (407) 885-5880

Career Development for Exceptional Individuals
   Council for Exceptional Children
   Division on Career Development
   1920 Association Drive
   Reston, VA 22091
   (703) 620-3660

Career Education News
   Bobit Publishing Company
   2500 Artesia Boulevard
   Redondo Beach, CA 90278

Career Planning and Adult Development Journal
   Career Planning and Adult Development
      Network
   1190 S. Bascom Avenue
   San Jose, CA 95128

Journal of Applied Rehabilitation Counseling
   633 S. Washington Street
   Alexandria, VA 22314

Journal of Career Development
   College of Education
   University of Missouri
   Columbus, MO 65211

Journal of Career Planning and Employment
   College Placement Council, Inc.
   62 Highland Avenue
   Bethlehem, PA 18017
   (215) 868-1421

Journal of Employment Counseling
   5999 Stevenson Avenue
   Alexandria, VA 22314

Journal of Postsecondary Education and
Disability
    P.O. Box 21192
    Columbus, OH 43221-0192
    (614) 488-4972

Journal of Rehabilitation
    633 S. Washington Street
    Alexandria, VA 22314

Journal of Rehabilitation Research
and Development
    103 Gay Street
    Baltimore, MD 12102
    (202) 745-8480

Journal of Vocational Behavior
    1250 Sixth Avenue
    San Diego, CA 92101

Journal for Vocational Special Needs Education
    University of Nebraska
    518 E. Nebraska Hall
    Lincoln, NE 68508-0515
    (402) 472-2365

Personnel and Guidance Journal
    American Association for Counseling &
      Development
    Two Skyline Place
    5203 Leesburg Pike
    Falls Church, VA 22041

Rehabilitation Counseling Bulletin
    5999 Stevenson Avenue
    Alexandria, VA 22304

Rehabilitation Education
    Pergamon Press, Journals Division
    Maxwell House
    Fairview Park
    Elmsford, NY 10523

Rehabilitation Psychology
    Springer Publishing Company
    536 Broadway
    New York, NY 10012

Rehabilitation World
    25 E. 21st Street
    New York, NY 10010

Vocational Education Journal
    1410 King Street
    Alexandria, VA 22314
    (703) 683-3111

Vocational Guidance Quarterly
    National Vocational Guidance Association
    Two Skyline Place
    5203 Leesburg Pike
    Falls Church, VA 22041

Professional Organizations, Advocacy Groups, and Other Information Sources

This section lists sources of information on topics related to components of life skills that include but are not limited to adolescent/adult services, employment of individuals with disabilities, transition, Individual Transition Plans, independent living, lifelong learning, vocational training, career education, rehabilitation, secondary special education, and work adjustment.

PROFESSIONAL ORGANIZATIONS

American Vocational Association
1410 King Street
Alexandria, VA 22314
(703) 683-3111;
(800) 826-9972

- National Association of Vocational Education Special Needs Personnel (NAVESNP)
- Special Needs Division

Association on Higher Education (AHEAD)
(Formerly the Association on Handicapped Student Services Programs in Post-Secondary Education [AHSSPPE])
P.O. Box 21192
Columbus, OH 43221
(614) 488-4972

Council for Exceptional Children
Division on Career Development and Transition
1920 Association Drive
Reston, VA 22091
(703) 620-3660

Council for Learning Disabilities
P.O. Box 40303
Overland Parks, KS 66204-4303
(913) 492-8755

Learning Disabilities Association of America (LDAA)
4156 Library Road
Pittsburg, PA 15234
(412) 341-1515

National Career Development Association
A Division of AACD
Publication Sales
5999 Stevenson Avenue
Alexandria, VA 22041

National Joint Committee on Learning Disabilities (NJCLD)
c/o Orton Dyslexia Society
724 York Road
Baltimore, MD 21204

National Rehabilitation Association
633 South Washington Street
Alexandria, VA 22314
(703) 836-0850

Vocational Evaluation and Work Adjustment Association
3600 Brakaw
Anchorage, AK 99508
(907) 333-2463

ADVOCACY GROUPS

President's Committee on Employment of People with Disabilities
1111 20th Street NW
Room 636
Washington, DC 20036-3470
(202) 653-5044

OTHER INFORMATION SERVICES

Americans with Disabilities Act Hotline
(800) USA-ABLE

ERIC Clearinghouse on Adult, Career, and Vocational Counseling
Ohio State University
Center on Education and Training for Employment
1900 Kenny Rd.
Columbus, OH 43210-1090
(614) 292-4353;
(800) 848-4815

Job Accommodations Network (JAN)
West Virginia University
809 Allen Hall
P.O. Box 6122
Morgantown, WV 26506
(800) 526-7234

Higher Education and Adult Training for People with Disabilities (HEATH)
1 Dupont Circle
Suite 8
Washington, DC 20036-1193
(202) 939-9320

National Center for Research in Vocational Education
Ohio State University
1960 Kenny Road
Columbus, OH 43210

**National Council of Independent Living
Programs (NCILP)**
Access Living
815 Van Buren
Suite 525
Chicago, IL 60607
(302) 226-5900

National Rehabilitation Information Center
8455 Colesville Road
Suite 935
Silver Spring, MD 20910-3319
(301) 588-9284

**National Resource Center for Materials on
Work Evaluation and Work Adjustments**
Materials Development Center
Stout Vocational Rehabilitation Institute
University of Wisconsin–Stout
Menomonie, WI 54751
(715) 232-1342

About the Authors...

Mary E. Cronin is Associate Professor of Special Education and Habilitative Services at the University of New Orleans. She has experience in teaching students with special needs at the preschool, elementary, and secondary levels. Her research interests include curriculum development, life skills instruction and materials development, behavior management, and secondary special needs program development. Her current interests include teacher training, life skills program development, and transition issues for students with mild disabilities. Mary received her BA from Avila College in Kansas City, Missouri, her MEd from the University of Kansas, and PhD from the University of Texas at Austin.

James R. Patton is the Executive Editor at PRO-ED and Adjunct Associate Professor at the University of Texas at Austin. He has experience teaching students with special needs at the elementary, secondary, and postsecondary levels. His research interests include curriculum development, lifelong learning, instructional methodology, and teaching science. Currently he is developing integrated curricula and life skills programs. Jim earned his BS from the University of Notre Dame and his MEd and EdD from the University of Virginia.